The Rabbi and the Widow

The Rabbi and the Widow

Charles David Isbell

INARA PUBLISHING

AN IMPRINT OF GCRR PRESS
1312 17TH STREET SUITE 549
DENVER, CO 80202

INFO@GCRR.ORG • INARAPUBLISHING.COM

Inara Publishing
An imprint of GCRR Press
1312 17th Street Suite 549
Denver, CO 80202
www.inarapublishing.com

Typesetting/Copyediting: Allison Guy
Cover Design: Darren M. Slade
Front Cover Image: Abdullah Al Mahmud
                    fiverr.com/mahmuddidar

Library of Congress Cataloging-in-Publication Data

The rabbi and the widow / Charles David Isbell
p.   cm.
ISBN (Paperback): 978-1-7362739-6-8
ISBN (eBook): 978-1-7362739-7-5
1. Widow—Judaism—Fiction.   2. Rabbi—Counseling—Fiction.   3. Marriage—Retirement—Fiction.   I. Title.

PN801-820   .I834   202

Contents

Prologue

I vory stretched her long legs toward the sun, luxuriating in the warmth that enveloped her as she exited the safety of the car.

Beginning with her first visit, the Louisiana landscape always had welcomed her, and she could sense the tensions of life being released as she strolled across the huge LSU campus, headed for the Quad. Spreading oak trees created a gentle pattern of shade-sun above the paved walkways and lush landscaping. Pink azaleas and purple crepe myrtles splashed color against the rich greenery, while the lemon scent of magnolia trees wafted through the balmy air.

Yes, she loved the university campus, but Ivory was a sun bunny, not a scholar, and she had come to enjoy the sun, the sights, and the scents.

Now, surrounded by classic southern ambiance and handsome, hundred-year-old buildings enclosing the Quad, Ivory lost herself in daydreams. This was the ideal setting for a picnic, and it perfectly suited her mood. Once the heart of campus life, the "Quad," as the Quadrangle had been known since its dedication in 1926, now offered a nostalgic look back at what was and what might have been.

Ivory was daydreaming about her first visit to LSU when Lilit intruded: "Ivory, what are you mooning about?"

"Oh, dear," thought Ivory. "Sunday mornings at LSU should be peaceful … and quiet."

But it was impossible to ignore Lilit, her friend, her protector, the huge, brindle Bullmastiff with the jutting underjaw that exposed her enormous white teeth. "Sometimes," Ivory thought, "Lilit looks like the hound from Hell." Only those who knew her well realized how gentle and loving she truly was.

The two friends were a study in contrasts. Alongside the fearsome Lilit, dainty Ivory looked like the picture of sweetness. But looks can be deceiving, and those who knew Ivory understood that the sleek, slim, all-white cat was wary and nervous, fearful of everything and everyone—likely because she was profoundly deaf. Only with her best friend close by could Ivory relax because she knew she would be safe.

Together, they ambled slowly across the lawn, finally arriving at the blanket on which the two others sat. They, too, were a study in contrasts. The man, Lilit's human, was rugged and serious. The lady who belonged to Ivory was graceful and elegant.

"Funny," thought Ivory, "I never realized how much Lilit resembles Dr. Broulliette. They both look fierce, but they are two of the gentlest souls a girl could ever meet."

Just then, Lilit was noticing that Sara and Ivory were also beautifully matched, slender, elegant, and demure.

Sensing each other's thoughts, Ivory and Lilit realized that they had arrived at the same conclusion about themselves: they both resembled their humans, at least in appearance. As they gazed at each other, Ivory reminisced. "Hey, Lilit, do you remember how they met?"

"Of course. I was there. And so were Jeff and Carlita a little bit later."

"It's a good thing all of us were there. Otherwise, no one would understand what really happened."

"I still find the story amazing," said Lilit. "We helped make miracles, didn't we?" She seemed lost in wonder at what she and her feline companion had accomplished.

For Lilit and Ivory, understanding each other did not require talking or a written word, two skills humans had invented because they just were not good at "communicating." All Lilit and Ivory needed to do to enjoy the story of "The Rabbi and the Widow" again was simple. They would start with the two humans who had recorded many of the details in the story—Jeff, a student who had studied with Dr. Broulliette and had written a journal with all kinds of information about his professor, and Carlita, Sara's beloved friend, girl Friday, and companion, who had gathered material about Sara from her unique perspective.

Without speaking a single human "word," both Ivory and Lilit would sail through Jeff's journal, plug in the chapter contributed by Carlita, and then race through the entire narrative about Rabbi Broulliette and Sara much quicker than a human could read.

Starting with Jeff's journal, here is the story that delighted them so much.

1

The Rabbi

Thirty students sat in various poses, some trying to look cool and composed, others fidgeting nervously in their seats, still others attempting to find something, anything, interesting in their stiff, new textbooks. They all looked up with a start when the professor entered. Even on a huge campus filled with unusual characters, this instructor stood out. Sixty-four years had not disguised his stocky frame or the boxer's forearms that emerged from his short-sleeved shirt, and although he did not move quickly, his gait was still somehow purposeful and athletic. His closely shaven head was crowned with a solid black *kippah*, and his grey beard seemed to have been woven from some form of thick underbrush. His eyes pierced the room, seemingly sizing up each of thirty individual students at once. He did not smile. He did not frown. His grizzled face was totally devoid of expression.

By far the most arresting feature of his physical appearance was the 110-pound Bullmastiff walking silently at his side wearing a jacket on which the words "***MEDIC ALERT***" appeared in bold letters. The service dog also scanned the class, her face equally lacking expression, and waited patiently as the professor placed his notebook on the podium and appeared to straighten a sheaf of papers. Turning to his massive companion, the professor spoke almost in a whisper. "*Lilit, Assis!*" Effortlessly, the dog sat erect facing the class, seeming to dare anyone to move. "*En bas*" was the next whisper, and the dog's huge frame settled into the prone position, her eyes never leaving the class.

The professor opened his notebook and addressed the class: "Good morning. I am Baraq Broulliette, and this is Introduction to Judaism." The voice was a rumbling bass, the eyes deep pools of brown, and the posture would have pleased a marine drill sergeant. Still there was no hint of a smile anywhere on his face.

From the back of the class, a nervous freshman silently mouthed the words, "We are going to die."

...

My name is Jeff. I was a senior that year, and Dr. Broulliette's class was the last general education course I needed to graduate with a major in psychology and human behavior. From the moment of Dr. Broulliette's entry into the classroom that morning, I determined that I had to learn what made this arresting-looking man tick. For the next five years, he and Lilit became my passion and ultimately the subject of my doctoral dissertation.

I got my first break when Lilit accepted me. In each class, she chose one student as her favorite, and I was the lucky winner in Introduction to Judaism that year. I assumed it was because I was seated in the front row and learned only later that any student in a wheelchair, as I was, automatically drew special attention from the service dog. Of course, the best part of being accepted by Lilit was that Dr. Broulliette was willing to spend more time with me. So, along with my formal doctoral research, I was able to incorporate into my collection of data the results of numerous conversations about scholarship, faith, and life. What follows is my compilation of those numerous conversations and many hours of research. I think you will find Dr. Broulliette as interesting a character as I do.

Thank God for the internet. I started with a simple Google search and quickly found the explanation for "Lilit." The details had appeared in the college newspaper five years earlier. Lilit was only a puppy when she was rescued from a kill shelter by the somber professor and then trained by him to act as a seizure alert dog for a high school student with epilepsy. In Dr. Broulliette's words, "She was the smartest dog I had ever met, and after only eight months of training, I thought she was almost ready to be placed with the epileptic youngster."

I had to ask: "How do you teach a dog to alert someone of an impending attack?"

"It's really quite simple," Dr. Broulliette responded, "but that does not make it easy." He then explained that dogs are able to hear the human heart beating, smell the chemical composition of the body, and know instantly when physiological changes are occurring.

The heartbeat is particularly significant. "A dog, even simply a family pet, automatically hears the heart beating," Dr. Broulliette explained, "and establishes a 'base rate' for each individual person with whom she is in frequent contact. When that base rate changes, the dog hears and reacts. Most people attach no significance to the behavior of the dog in such moments and thus fail to understand what is perfectly clear to her. But once human handlers learn to observe what the dog does when a heart rate changes, the dog becomes an early indication of impending troubles—a seizure, a heart attack or stroke, even simply a sudden spell of dizziness."

"So," he continued, "I start by placing a small kitchen timer on my chest. Its ticks generate a rhythm that is distinct from the heartbeat. All dogs can hear it, of course, but most will simply cock their heads and perk their ears out of curiosity. The first time I tried it with Lilit, she jumped immediately onto the couch with me and began to whine, wanting me to know that something did not sound right to her. I knew then that she was a keeper."

I recalled the actions of my own family pet that had always seemed to sense when I had the flu or trouble breathing with bronchitis. "Exactly," said Dr. Broulliette enthusiastically. "But you did not respond to her signals. The trick is not teaching the dog to notice what is happening but to train the human to interpret the manner in which the dog reacts to what it is experiencing. Every time Lilit seems to be disobeying, I replay in my mind what has happened and always realize that I have overlooked some change in her behavior. She is always right."

In fact, Dr. Broulliette admitted, "My failure to trust her almost cost me my life."

Seeing my puzzled look, he continued. "Shortly before Lilit was due to be delivered to her epileptic patient, I awakened early one morning feeling terribly ill and assumed it was something I had eaten the night before. When I took Lilit outside, she began to disobey—the proper word is 'override'—every command I gave her, and I grew irritated because she had never disobeyed before. Refusing even to relieve herself, she alternately growled and pawed at my legs until she forced me to sit in a patio chair. Once I was seated, she continued to override my commands, continued to whine and growl, and finally reared up to place both giant paws on my thighs, refusing to let me stand from my chair. Then, she literally crashed her ear directly to my chest, trying to tell me what she was hearing. At first I was unable to believe that the dog was warning *me*, but I finally made a cautionary call to a medical doctor friend, who, hearing my answers to his questions about respiration and chest and arm pains, called for an ambulance to transport me to the hospital."

I listened in amazement as Dr. Broulliette described his arrival at the emergency room, the oxygen mask, the nitro-glycerin pack, the monitors, and the presence of a cardiologist in the room with him. Only four minutes after arriving at the emergency room, he suffered a massive heart attack that surely would have taken his life at home—except home was where Lilit ruled, and her human was not going to die while she was on duty. Wheeled into the operating theater after surviving the attack, Dr. Broulliette had undergone angioplasty, during which titanium stints were implanted into his arteries. Only five days later, the professor returned home to cradle the powerful dog in his arms, to apologize for having doubted her, and to promise that never again would they be separated. He agreed to train another dog for the epileptic youngster, of course. But from that day, the professor and Lilit were always together.

Google yielded scores of other entries, most of them the kind to be expected for a professor with a long career—five university degrees including two doctorates, ten technical books, something more than two hundred articles in learned journals, countless scholarly papers at academic conferences—the list was long and impressive. But the numbers told only part of the story. Unlike many academicians, the professor was not just an expert in one small area of arcane knowledge. Over a period of more than thirty years, Dr. Broulliette had written extensively about an astonishing variety of subjects and issues: the grammar and syntactical structure of several different languages, history, biblical literature, philosophy of religion, theology, Middle Eastern archaeology, Jewish liturgy. He was an ordained rabbi and an invested cantor as well as a scholar and teacher. He spoke seven modern languages fluently, read a dozen ancient languages and scripts, had taught at two other large universities, had lived in three other countries (Germany, Israel, Iraq), and had served for two years as the epigraphist for an archaeological excavation team. Each country had left an indelible impression on him, and I became curious about his impressions of the countries in which he had resided.

When I asked him about Germany, his response included a story that shocked and saddened me. Planning to spend a full twelve months in the country, Dr. Broulliette had begun with a two-month crash course in conversational German at a famous Goethe-Institut near Cologne to prepare for two full semesters of literature courses at Bonn University under a well-known German Protestant professor of Old Testament literature. When the school year ended, Dr. Broulliette still had one month remaining on his visa and decided to tour the country. His first stop was in nearby Cologne. Standing outside the famous Cologne cathedral, he overheard a German couple standing behind him discussing the bullet marks that still pocked the beautiful structure. Their remarks scathingly decried the American bombing of a stunning architectural landmark. Dr. Broulliette, then only twenty-two years old, finally turned to them and asked in German, "Who started the war?" In his words, "I saw a look of hatred unlike anything I had ever experienced. The man's face morphed into a mangle of pinched nerves as he spat out his answer: '*Die Jüden*!' ('The Jews!'). I was so shocked and angered by the answer and the hatred that prompted it that I left the next day, refusing to spend another minute in the country that had visited such unspeakable anguish on my people."

Dr. Broulliette was soft-spoken and deliberate most of the time, but his recall of this one incident revealed that he was in fact a deeply emotional man whose feelings about his people were neither hidden nor ambiguous.

"Yes," he had admitted, "I learned a lot about the literature of the Hebrew Bible, but I also discovered the anti-Semitic leanings of some of Germany's most famous professors of the Bible whose erudition I had previously admired. This knowledge soured me on Germany, and I have never been back."

Our next conversation was about Iraq, and I assumed Dr. Broulliette would be equally dismissive of Arab Muslims. I was surprised at his assessment of them. "They are a wonderful people," he said pensively, "and they have suffered from terrible leadership for most of the past century. Perhaps best of all," he remarked with a broad smile, "they know how to season their food properly."

I waited for another story and was not disappointed.

"At supper on my first night with the archaeological team in Iraq, the locals who cooked for us prepared a simple falafel dish, which they dutifully placed on my plate as I came through the line. I had never seen falafel before, and I hesitated with what must have been a quizzical look on my face. The server took a large ladle, filled it with a bright red sauce, and held it up, asking, '*Harif*?' I had no idea what '*harif*' was, and I knew only that the Arabic word meant 'sharp.' I figured I should try whatever they offered and answered '*Na'am*' ('Yes'), so he covered my falafel with it. I noticed that the serving staff followed me with their eyes as I found a table, and I realized that they were watching me take my first bite of *harif*. It was the tangiest, hottest sauce in the land and reminded me of the seasonings my family had always added to food, so I enjoyed every bite, not realizing why the staff seemed delighted when I asked for a second serving. I did not yet know that no other archaeologist had even tried *harif*, and I had no idea that my eating habits made such an impression on the cooks. But I decided that night that I could relate to any people who produced such delicious food."

Dr. Broulliette had several other stories about the customs of the local people among whom he had worked, and his description of them was unfailingly complimentary. I was not surprised to learn that he still corresponded with several Iraqi friends he had made almost thirty years earlier.

I asked him next about Israel, and Dr. Broulliette paused for several moments before responding. "Well," he said softly, "they are my people. I fought in two wars with them, and I feel in Israel that I am home. But I am an American by birth, and this is where I belong. Israel doesn't need Hebrew teachers, but America does. So, I have remained in America."

Digging through a stack of scholarly journals in the university library, I found a thirty-year-old picture of Dr. Broulliette taken in Iraq. Back then, his thick beard had been black, his head already well on its way to becoming completely bald. The article containing his picture was a preliminary report of the discovery of a large number of clay food bowls found in an ancient palace. Each tablet contained some kind of magical incantation written by Jewish magicians in ancient Aramaic, and Dr. Broulliette had translated the entire cache for the team on which he served. They were the first scholarly articles he had published.

His explanation about the "magic bowls," the incantations written on plain food bowls, was intriguing and enlightening. Most scholars of Judaism focus on the standard literature of the first few Christian centuries, the Talmud. Here are found the discussions of life and law and faith carried on among the Jewish scholars of the era, and many students of Judaism look to the Talmud for information about true Judaism as it was perceived by these great masters. But at the same time the Jewish creators of the Talmud were debating among themselves the great questions of life and faith, average Jews traveled another avenue in their pursuit of an appropriate way of life. Magic was an essential element in their pursuit.

"You see," Dr. Broulliette explained, "most people believed that in addition to the physical world experienced through sensory perception, an alternate universe of the spirit world existed, no less real because it was unseen."

It was indeed an alternate explanation of reality. Spirits that exist in this "alternate universe" were believed to be in control of virtually all facets of life in the physical universe. Some of these spirits were good, but some were evil, and their existence helped explain to common people various negative aspects of daily life. Although such a view embodies the very type of dualism that standard Judaism vehemently denies with respect to God, it was useful for ordinary folk.

Furthermore, the "alternate universe" exhibited its own unique structure, tying each spirit to its own particular guild. According to Jewish legend, a lilit-demon/spirit named Piznai had become infatuated with the beauty of Adam, tricked him into a sexual union, and subsequently bore a host of both male and female demons, so many that their offspring filled the entire unseen world of the spirit. Because she was incapable of bearing *human* children for Adam, he had divorced her to marry Eve, who became the mother of all humanity. It was only natural that the original Lilit and all her offspring would bear deep hatred for Eve and her human progeny.

So, in Jewish folklore, Eve was not the first wife of Adam. That honor had belonged to "Lilit," whose very name implies darkness or "night." The fate of all human females was tied to the activities of the spirits that comprise the special group of *liliyata* ("lilits"). Some good spirits in the group could attempt to assist women in their lives, including strategic events like childbirth, illness, or moments of physical danger. But there were mostly evil spirits in the mix, and their goal was to torment and harm women at every possible turn in the road.

The methods of these offspring of the original Lilit and Adam were insidious and evil, and Dr. Broulliette furnished an unforgettable example. "Suppose that a nice Jewish couple has a terrible child, disobedient and fractious. Such a child obviously could not have sprung from two good parents (!). Instead, a male *lili* (the masculine spelling of the word) must have morphed itself into the shape of the husband (an *incubus*) in order to copulate with the wife (whose marital faithfulness is fully assumed), and it was his demon seed that had infested the terrible child."

As I scribbled notes frantically, Dr. Broulliette continued. "A female *lilit* could also transform herself into the exact duplicate of the wife (a *succubus*) in order to copulate with the innocent husband. Then, she would return to the wilderness to have the child, and the demon offspring would naturally seek to find its father. Her search could explain innumerable incidents that threatened the safety of the nice Jewish home: rattling window shutters, mysteriously disappearing items, unexplained broken dishes or furniture, even a preponderance of headaches or other physical ailments."

In all such instances, Dr. Broulliette explained, "the innocence of the Jewish parents was safeguarded, but an explanation for the oddities of existence was offered."

So, how do simple people combat such forces? Enter the magician, whose skill Dr. Broulliette compared only partially facetiously to that of the modern psychiatrist. "He knew all about the lilits, male and female, and he understood their origins from the original Lilit and Adam. When called upon, he could write a protective incantation that would inhibit the ability of the offending spirit to harm the family."

"Writing, of course, made the document official. But the magician had to appeal to the authority of the guild leader, demanding that she order the lower-ranking member who was the actual cause of the problem to cease and desist. The practitioner could not simply write an incantation containing an open appeal to Lilit, the guild head. He would have to write her name in a secret, magical spelling that she could not undo with her own black magic."

I remembered that an early scholarly article by Dr. Broulliette was an explanation of the various ways in which the name of Lilit could be permuted in spelling so that she could not recognize and undo the authority that was compelling her, and assumed that I had just learned the significance of Dr. Broulliette's service dog's name. When I mentioned the connection, he noted with twinkling eyes: "No, I chose her name for another reason. She is like her master. She looks tough on the outside, but inside, she is all heart and sweetness. In fact, she is a true sabra."

Noting my puzzled look, Dr. Broulliette explained that a "sabra" is a cactus plant that is rough on the exterior but sweet to the taste once its prickly outer cover has been removed. For this dual reason, it is believed to be quite an accurate description of the modern Israeli: rough and ready for action but loyal and kind to friends. Seeing Dr. Broulliette and Lilit together, I was convinced that they were two real-life examples of a sabra.

Dr. Broulliette and I discussed many other articles he had written through the years, and that was how I became familiar with his vast range of knowledge mentioned earlier. But far down the list provided by Google, I uncovered a fact that seemed to belong to the life of a different person. As a young man, Dr. Broulliette had spent two years handling a bomb-sniffing dog for the IDF, followed by a third year as a military canine trainer.

Dr. Broulliette was reluctant at first to discuss his career in the Israeli military. But one afternoon in his office, he suggested that he could use a drink and asked if I would like to accompany him. Over his second glass of wine, more relaxed than I had ever seen him, he began to speak. "For three years in the military, a dog was my constant companion. We ate, slept, and worked together every single day, and anyone who thinks animals are incapable of love simply has never given a dog a fair chance."

Noting that Dr. Broulliette's hand was gently caressing the massive head of Lilit, I waited silently for him to continue. "You know, we humans are terribly arrogant. We assume that we are the most important animal in the forest, and in truth, we are in many ways. Yet every creature is special, and those we have managed to domesticate and turn into working partners are quite invaluable to us."

After another sip of wine, he almost whispered. "More than once, my military dog saved my life. And now, Lilit has done that too. I owe these beautiful critters more than I can ever repay."

When I pressed him for details, he simply said, "Twice I started to enter a building that we assumed had been cleared of explosives, but each time, my canine partner refused to allow me to move. Both times, we backed away from the entrance only seconds before the explosion that would have killed us both. They knew. I did not."

Sensing that there was more to the story, I waited. He abruptly turned his back to me and turned to face me directly only after several awkward moments of silence. I noticed two silver tears trickling down his rough cheeks that he refused to wipe away. "Once," and now he *was* whispering, "my partner jumped over a retainer wall rather than let me do it because she could not convince me to stop. The explosion killed her instantly. I never have forgiven myself for failing to listen to her signal." I was stunned at the inner tenderness no longer hidden behind the external appearance of the serious professor.

An academician who had served in the military with bomb-sniffing dogs, an animal lover who continued to train dogs as service companions for handicapped youngsters, including the faithful partner that now enabled him to lead a normal life! I decided to dig deeper. How had an ex-IDF canine handler become a rabbi, a cantor, a scholar who compiled an extensive academic background? What had brought him to LSU? And how had he become the man I was now studying?

The Early Years

The year was 1944. Millions of Jews were still imprisoned all over Eastern Europe by the Nazi regime; thousands were being sent to gas chambers daily. Far away, in Cajun-speaking south Louisiana, a simple farm wife served as the midwife for an entire parish that lacked a hospital or a single full-time doctor. Returning to her own tiny farmhouse as midnight approached late one August evening, Agnes Broulliette fought the fatigue that an eighteen-hour delivery had occasioned. Without bothering to eat supper, she fell into her own bed and immediately slept the sleep of the exhausted. She had spoken only one sentence to her family upon her return: "If anyone disturbs me, they'll wish they had never been born."

A mere three hours later, her husband's gruff voice shouted, "Agnes, get up. It's Josephine." Agnes was fully alert immediately. Josephine was her only daughter, the apple of her father's eye, and the first member of the family to have graduated from college.

How, thought Agnes, could things have gone so wrong? Josephine—beautiful, intelligent Josephine—had met a young man at college and had become pregnant by him. In 1944, such a thing was scandalous. But it quickly became worse. Upon learning the news of her pregnancy, the man, whose name Agnes refused to utter, had sneered, "I'm not marrying any Jew" and promptly disappeared. Abandoned and humiliated, Josephine had crept home to the safety of her parents and resolutely determined that she would make a good life for her child and herself.

Snatching her midwife's kit from the dresser, Agnes hurried upstairs to Josephine's bedroom, finding her daughter bathed in perspiration and writhing with the pain of impending delivery. Almost before Agnes could open her medical bag, the baby's head appeared, and within seconds, the robust boy began to scream in protest against being forced from the warm and safe cocoon of his mother's womb.

"Baraq," said the new grandfather who was observing silently. "The rascal moves like lightning." In this cacophonous fashion did the child whom I would later meet as Dr. Broulliette begin life in this world.

When Dr. Broulliette told me the story, he chuckled. "Of course, my folks were all Cajun Jews, so I'm fairly certain they added a few salacious details to the drama."

One of only two Jewish families in the predominantly Catholic parish, the Broulliette clan included young Baraq's mother, grandparents, four uncles and aunts, and eleven cousins born in the ten years following the arrival of Dr. Broulliette. Together, the extended family comprised a small polyglot enclave. Grandmother Agnes spoke Yiddish with her sisters and French with everyone else; the grandfather spoke French to everyone except his grandson, with whom he spoke only in Hebrew. Baraq's mother, Josephine, served as teacher of French at a local high school and was the only family member conversant in English. Thus, the medium of communication changed for young Baraq depending on his adult caretaker for the day. By the age of four, he could converse easily in four languages.

But languages were not the only diverse aspect of the Broulliette family. Baraq's grandfather not only maintained a small forty-acre farm—he also ran a "general store" in the days before Walmart made such entities no longer profitable. And "Monsieur B," as he was known affectionately, established a reputation for hard work, honesty, and square dealing. He was also widely recognized as one of the funniest men in the area, putting an original stamp on his own brand of Cajun country humor.

When a customer asked him the price of a pair of brogans, the hardy work boots of laborers in the area, he replied that they cost three dollars.

"But Mr. Juneau sells them for *two* dollars," the customer protested.

"Well, go buy them from Mr. Juneau" was the response.

"But he's all out of brogans," said the customer.

"Me, when I'm out of brogans," noted Monsieur B, "I *give* 'em away!"

"Miss Agnes" was no less notable. In addition to her parish-wide service as a midwife, she was renowned for her baking prowess, especially coconut cakes. But while her cakes melted in the mouth, her temper was pure acid. The woman who thought nothing of sitting up all night with a frightened delivering mom made no attempt to hold her tongue when provoked. Once, given the wrong directions to a house where she was to deliver a baby, she promptly retraced her path for the single purpose of finding the culprit whose directions had misled her. "Mais God damn, but you stupid" was her verdict, shouted directly into the face of the miscreant. Her anger vented, she proceeded to the right house and delivered a healthy baby girl.

Perhaps the outstanding Broulliette family characteristic was a determined intensity that was often labeled as stubbornness. Miss Josephine, needing to borrow money in order to open an insurance agency, was denied because she did not have a male co-signer. When Mr. B volunteered to sign with his daughter, she refused his offer, threatened the reluctant banker with a lawsuit, and obtained the loan. The year was 1950, long before the days of the feminist movement. These characteristics of hard work, humor, explosive temper, and steely resolve all seemed to pass directly to young Baraq.

At the age of four, Baraq had his first encounter with the law. During a trip to town for supplies, Mr. B turned his attention to a purchase for only a moment, and Baraq was gone. He was discovered minutes later standing in the middle of the busiest intersection in town, and adults watched in amazement and horror as the sturdy waif did his best to direct traffic, motioning one car to turn left, to another, granting permission to turn right, and then to a short line of waiting vehicles giving the signal to proceed through the intersection. Snatched to safety by a concerned motorist who stopped alongside him, Baraq remained the picture of calm throughout. Even a stern lecture from a worried city cop failed to dim his enthusiasm or his conviction that he was quite capable of directing traffic. Mr. B could only shake his head.

In 1950, before preschools and kindergarten, Baraq entered grade one in the public school system, where his first teacher quickly recognized the range of personality features that distinguished her newest student: he possessed amazing linguistic skills, he could reduce an entire class to laughter with outrageously funny remarks, and—he was acutely aware that he was "different." A Jew in a Catholic environment, a fatherless boy among tightly knit families, a country boy sent to school in "town," Baraq learned early to fight in response to insults hurled in English or French. Once, succeeding in landing only a few blows before being soundly thrashed by an older boy, young Baraq remarked simply: "Well, at least it cost him *something* to call me a son of a bitch."

1950 also marked another major change in Baraq's life. His mother moved to a larger town to open a small insurance agency with the bank loan, and the boy was left with his grandparents on the farm. Baraq's first hero was his grandfather, a secular Jew who looked upon organized religion as a curse and never attended synagogue services (the closest one was more than thirty miles away, an impossible distance for a family in those days). Yet, Mr. B clung doggedly to several Jewish traditions and culture. Although he was never told why, young Baraq always knew that his family did not eat pork or shellfish, that his grandmother lit candles on Friday evening, and that his grandfather kept a special knife used only for severing the carotid artery of an animal that he butchered. No one spoke of any religious reason for these customs; they were simply a part of daily life.

Riding on a tractor with Mr. B, Baraq watched as his grandfather abruptly stopped and then steered a careful course around a clump of growth. As they passed the clump, Baraq noted the mother dove and her babies ensconced in their nest shielded by the surrounding growth. "They have the right to live too," Mr. B remarked quietly, and Baraq never forgot the incident.

Nor could he fail to notice that during harvest, Mr. B never cut the corners of a field of grain. "Too much trouble" was the simple explanation from Mr. B, and Baraq learned only much later that an entire tractate of the Talmud is devoted to the requirement that harvesters leave uncut the corners of a field so that poor people could be allowed to glean for their daily subsistence.

He also learned the hard way that dishonesty and untruth were never tolerated. Visiting a small grocery store in town with his grandfather, young Baraq filched a candy bar while the store owner spoke with Mr. B. When his grandfather discovered the boy eating the stolen goods at home, the two Broulliette males promptly returned to the store to face the owner, who was still unaware of Baraq's act. Red-faced, with a glowering grandfather standing by in a threatening pose, Baraq admitted his crime and agreed to sweep the store every afternoon for a week in exchange for the candy bar. On the way home, Mr. B uttered only one short sentence: "Jews don't steal, Baraq, and they don't lie." Baraq never stole again, and he never lied to his grandfather.

In his stern grandfather, Baraq found the male role model that every small boy needs for another aspect of life. Mr. B's imprint on the boy was also unmistakable with respect to his capacity for hard work. Even for a small boy, chores on the farm began when the rooster crowed and continued until sunset. Before breakfast, young Baraq worked to clean the barn, helped milk cows by hand, fed the family chickens and gathered their eggs, and made certain that all the dogs and cats had fresh water and food. During the summer, he worked alongside his grandfather at the endless variety of tasks demanded by a farm. After supper, in a home that contained no television set, he sat on the porch chatting with his grandmother and her sisters in Yiddish while shelling pecans or hulling peas, or speaking Hebrew as he helped his grandfather sharpen a saw or repair a piece of furniture or a simple tool. Failure to do one's share of the work was not an option.

Mixed with the stern demeanor of his grandfather, Baraq detected what many who knew the man only casually may not have realized. Whether making soup for a sick friend, caring for a wounded or abandoned animal, or helping a neighbor repair his barn, Monsieur B never let an opportunity to perform a "*mitzvah*" pass. Even here, Mr. B's caustic wit never failed. Gruffly handing a pot of chicken soup to an ill neighbor, he brushed away the proffered thanks of the grateful wife. "Ah, Terese, as bad as your cooking is, Baptiste would never get well. And he owes me for last month's supplies." The small grandson smiled, but in fact, Mr. B's actions in such situations defined the word *mitzvah* itself for Baraq. These multiple acts of kindness and generosity made a deep impression on the young lad, matched repeatedly once Baraq became an adult.

His second hero was a piano teacher who agreed to teach him in exchange for light chores around her house. Baraq's passion for music, born of his need for an energy outlet, proved to be his salvation. Whenever he was left alone while his grandmother delivered a baby and Monsieur B minded the store, the piano became his best friend, and it was quickly evident that his musical talents matched his linguistic ability.

But here, too, his independence surfaced. During a piano recital, Baraq was scheduled to play a piece of modest difficulty which the teacher was certain he could do flawlessly. To her surprise, Baraq began to play an entirely different and much more difficult piece, one to which he had been introduced only a few weeks earlier. His performance was not flawless, but he managed. Defending himself after the recital, sixth-grader Baraq said simply, "What's the point of doing something that is easy?" The teacher had no reply, she but began from that moment to push Baraq harder than she had ever pushed any other student.

During the summer preceding his eighth year in school, Baraq's grandmother died, and the young boy went with his grandfather to join his mother. The small house in Josephine's larger town lacked the open fields that had surrounded Baraq's first home, and the new school produced fresh insults, calling forth the violent response he had perfected long ago. But this time, the social problems were accompanied by academic and legal troubles. Baraq's grades plummeted, and he was returned to his mother in the custody of an officer of the law more than once. Baraq and fighting became linked.

Baraq's stepfather, who had married his mother three years earlier, decided that the boy needed discipline. His stern lectures soon escalated to corporal punishment, and the boy who had known tough love from his first male role model, but never corporal punishment, now experienced the back of a grown man's hand to his face for the first time. Partially because he was jealous of his wife's affection for Baraq, but largely because he stupidly believed he was saving the boy, the stepfather, whose name Baraq refused to utter as Agnes had refused to utter the name of Baraq's biological father, increased the level of violence against his stepson, frequently whipping him with his leather belt.

At the age of fifteen, the boy who had learned early to respond to insults from classmates by fighting finally reacted physically against his stepfather, landing a hard blow to the older man's face. But the man was far heavier and more powerful than the budding teen, and the result was a serious beating for Baraq. His nose was broken, one eye was closed and blackened, and two ribs were cracked. In those days, of course, no one turned to child protection agencies in such cases. The stepfather reported his own version of the incident to Baraq's mother, and when her son refused to say a word about it, she was left with no option but to accept her husband's explanation that the boy had attacked him and to pray that the boy had learned his lesson.

Only the grandfather heard the complete story from Baraq, but he refused to excuse the actions of his grandson. "You never sass an adult, Baraq," he said quietly, "Even when he is wrong."

Baraq was never told about the ensuing conversation between the offending stepfather and Mr. B. But the beatings stopped.

Inevitably, of course, Baraq was arrested on a more serious charge—inciting a brawl by breaking the jaw of an opponent in the parking lot of the local bowling alley, where all the high school kids "hung out." This time, there would be more than a lecture from a finger-wagging local cop, and Baraq found himself standing in the city courtroom facing a judge whose own son was Baraq's best and only friend. Outwardly defiant, struggling to ignore his tearful mother seated in the front row, Baraq was certain that his friend's father would go easy on him. The words "Ninety days in the parish youth prison" sent him into mild shock.

Hope and relief flooded Baraq's mind when the burly police officer who had arrested him stepped forward. "Your honor, I would like for this boy to be remanded to my custody. I will take full responsibility for his behavior."

But the relief Baraq felt soon dissipated. The officer, a former marine boxer, spoke bluntly on the courthouse steps. "Look, kid, I'm your only chance. Since you are so tough, I will teach you how to fight properly, and you can test yourself against other tough guys in a ring with a referee and rules. Mess with me, and your Jewish butt lands behind bars."

The 160-pound teenager sized up the 240-pound officer and decided that he was overmatched. So, the boxing lessons began. But as Baraq found an outlet for his aggression, he discovered something quite important. He was fearless, but he was not particularly skilled as a boxer. He won most of his fights on sheer grit but always seemed to take too many punches and seldom felt like a true victor. Realizing that he would never be the middleweight champion of the world, and knowing that the officer would cut him no slack, Baraq was determined to develop his other skills. Good grades were one product of his new outlook on life, as was a renewed devotion to his beloved piano. When he turned sixteen, his mother gave permission for him to play the piano at a hotel restaurant nearby, and he began saving money for college.

But Baraq was not content simply to play at the restaurant and accept the standard wage. He found a large brandy snifter and placed it on the piano with several bills from his own pocket clearly visible. In short order, his tips often exceeded his salary, and his savings began to grow.

And then, Baraq discovered romance. As the star of French class, Baraq was sought by other students as a partner for class projects and assignments. When a dark-eyed beauty named Janice asked him to help her with an assignment, Baraq was smitten. Janice was the daughter of the local Methodist minister, and she and Baraq could not have been more different. Baraq was bouncy and almost arrogant around people, but with Janice, he became painfully shy. Janice, who was normally shy and soft-spoken around everyone else, quickly became light-hearted and free with Baraq. When she initiated their first kiss, Baraq's world changed, and as he recalled the moment to his mother, from whom he kept no secrets, his description captured the essence of what only young lovers know: "I could not breathe. My face flushed, and my knees buckled."

Josephine seized the opportunity for a serious talk, and Baraq learned for the first time a few of the details of his mother's relationship with his biological donor. Watching his reaction, and seeing realization dawn in his eyes, Josephine believed that Baraq would have the fortitude to avoid the terrible mistake she had made during her first foray into romance. She was right, but little did she know that Baraq would speak bluntly with Janice, assuring her of his love, while procuring her agreement that they had to be careful. Baraq and Janice remained a couple for their final two years in school together but never ventured into the sexual liaison that could have altered their young lives. And little did Baraq know of how grateful Janice was to be relieved of the awful pressure most young girls feel to "prove" their love.

Upon being graduated from high school, the determined teen was granted a music scholarship to a small Methodist college in Oklahoma. He learned only much later that the father of his beautiful Janice, the local Methodist minister, had recommended him for the scholarship. Janice earned an academic scholarship to a different college, and the two sweethearts were separated. As often happens, their teenaged passion did not survive their separation.

College Man, Cantor

Once his college days began, Baraq soon learned that he was still "different." He had no interest in the religious tenets of the college, did not drink alcohol or play cards, and made few friends among the other students. While they partied, Baraq played piano at an upscale steak house nearby, still saving his money carefully and living simply. While most students took the easiest courses available, Baraq declared a triple major in classics, music, and religion.

Told that he needed a modern foreign language to graduate, Baraq enrolled in a Russian class. When he overheard his Russian teacher, who was the wife of the French professor, conversing with her husband in French, he joined in the conversation.

"Why are you taking Russian, Baraq," he was asked, "when you already are fluent in French?"

"Well," replied the simple country boy, "I was told that I needed a *foreign* language to graduate!"

Midway through the first semester of his freshman year, unable to return home for the Thanksgiving holidays, Baraq wandered aimlessly through the streets of downtown Oklahoma City and spotted a synagogue, the first one he had ever seen. Greeted by the seventy-eight-year-old rabbi as he entered, he felt oddly at home for the first time in his young life. The rabbi was amazed to find a young boy who spoke Hebrew fluently and made a decision that would change Baraq's life forever.

"A music major with flawless Hebrew! So, you'll be our cantor."

The rabbi became Baraq's third hero. Attending services of worship for the first time, tutored by the rabbi in the intricacies of Jewish liturgy, Baraq proved a willing pupil who absorbed the wisdom of the rabbi and begged for more. Less than two weeks after setting foot in a synagogue for the first time, Baraq assisted the rabbi as he led prayer services in Hebrew, to the delight of his new spiritual family. He plunged enthusiastically into active Jewish life, serving the aging and dwindling congregation in need of a young and talented cantor to lead services of worship. On Saturday mornings, while his college mates lingered in bed after late nights on the town, Baraq sang the melodies of Jewish prayer, finding in the ancient words new meaning for his own young life. Surrounded by people whose lives were grounded in Jewish worship and wisdom, Baraq began to develop a sense of his own identity that had remained out of reach as long as he had been the only Jewish boy in a Christian high school.

As music had led him to discover his Jewishness, so now languages and music led him to academic excellence. He redoubled his efforts at mastering the piano, began voice lessons, and studied music history, theory, and composition. In his religion classes, he began to learn about the philosophical framework of Christianity, and he was introduced to other great faith systems around the world. To complete the classics component of his tripartite major, Baraq added Greek and Latin to his arsenal. By his senior year, he began to serve as the teaching assistant in Greek and Latin—and French!

During the second semester of his senior year, Baraq was called to the office of the registrar and informed by a strait-laced office worker that he could not graduate because he had not declared a "minor." Only the intervention of the college registrar himself allowed Baraq to skirt the rules, and thereafter, Baraq often reminded his friends that he had never completed a minor in college—only three majors!

Baraq finished his undergraduate education in three years, and he stayed at the college to pursue a master's degree in classics. At the age of twenty-one, he wrote a master's thesis on Greek literature that marked him as a coming star.

Israel and First Love

Upon his graduation in 1966, Baraq embarked for Israel and began living with a Jewish family that had emigrated from Iraq, adding Arabic to his arsenal of languages. Early in 1967, he received a job offer to serve as an instructor of biblical languages at a small Methodist seminary in Kansas City. Because he had no other option, he decided to accept and purchased a ticket to return to America in late summer. But the Six-Day War of June 1967 interrupted his plans. Baraq became a dual Israeli-American citizen and enlisted in the IDF, where he was assigned to a canine unit.

1967 was also the year when Baraq met Leora, a fourth-generation Israeli beauty who stole his heart. Just before the outbreak of the war, as they discussed their plans for marriage, Leora confided to Baraq her desire to study in the United States, and she promised to return with him when his three-year military tour ended. Baraq's future seemed to have changed for the better.

But Leora was also in the Israeli military, service that was compulsory for male and female citizens. The stray bullet that pierced the heart of Leora several months after the end of the war also shattered Baraq's world. Haunted by the loss of Leora, he spent the following three years completing his military tour and studying at a well-known Yeshiva in his spare time, permitting himself no opportunity for social development or making new friends. In June 1970, Baraq was discharged from the army and graduated from the Yeshiva, accepting ordination as a rabbi.

But he still had no job, no plans, and no vision for his future. When the seminary offer was renewed, he returned to the USA and accepted the position as instructor of Greek, Latin, and Hebrew.

Home, Faith, and a Third Love

The advice of his beloved grandfather caused Baraq to rethink the priorities of his life. As had many other Jews before him, Baraq considered the advantages of living as a Christian in a

Christian-dominated society. The old man was convinced that Judaism was destined to die out in America, to be replaced by Christianity. And he believed Baraq would have no future as a rabbi. Swayed by Mr. B's advice, Baraq decided not only to perform his teaching role but also to enroll in the seminary course of study leading to the doctorate in Christian theology, supporting himself by his assignment as instructor of biblical languages. Yet, as he had done in Oklahoma City, in Kansas City as well, he served a small downtown synagogue as a cantor.

During the summer preceding his graduation from seminary, Baraq, presumed by the committee in charge of assignments to be a Christian, was invited to join a team of scholars who were issuing a modern English translation of the Bible. One of the other committee members was James Younger, a Christian professor of the Old Testament at a liberal American Baptist seminary. Watching the younger man work with the other translators, Dr. Younger was amazed at his linguistic skills, his energy, and his willingness to work long hours at a grueling task. The older man and young Baraq developed a warm friendship, and Baraq listened as Dr. Younger regaled him with stories of his own days as a graduate student. And Baraq was fascinated to learn that his new friend had earned his PhD in the quintessentially Jewish environment of Dropsie College in Philadelphia. His doctoral advisor had been Cyrus Gordon, one of the most famous scholars of Judaism in the twentieth century. The idea of studying with a Jewish scholar who was liberal enough to teach Christian students captured Baraq's imagination.

Now fully conflicted, Baraq sought advice both from his rabbi and colleague at the synagogue and his new Christian mentor. Throughout the final year of his doctoral program at the seminary, writing a dissertation on New Testament quotations of the Old Testament, he seemed trapped between the two sides of his social and religious conflict. The values by which many of his Christian acquaintances lived seemed to him quite similar to the values he had learned from his grandfather. And the conservative Christian culture of Kansas City did seem to indicate that Judaism was on the wane. But the Christian tradition of interpreting the Hebrew Scriptures through the lens of the New Testament bothered him, and he was drawn to the Talmudic rabbinic debates that placed the ancient sacred texts in the service of modern Jewish life. It was the Christian professor who opened Baraq's eyes.

"You are not a Christian, Baraq," Dr. Younger noted gently, "and you should not try to become what you are not. You know the profundity of Judaism. What is more, it speaks to you as the New Testament has failed to do. You must learn to be comfortable in your own skin."

Baraq realized that the wise professor was correct. Having looked openly at the two ways of approaching theological truth, Baraq admitted to himself that he was not, and never could be, a believing Christian. Judaism was meaningful to him, and he believed it was a pathway to God that retained its own independent integrity, perhaps not for everyone but for him. Whether he liked it or not, he was a Jew. He decided to accept the responsibilities of his ordination as a rabbi, and he explained to the seminary faculty that he would not seek ordination as a Methodist minister. With a strong recommendation from Dr. Younger added to his outstanding academic record, Baraq received a scholarship to Brandeis University to study classical Judaism with Dr. Gordon.

But the theological conflict was not the only issue with which Baraq was forced to wrestle. The haunting image of Lyn stared him in the face. His third true love could not be denied, but the fact that she was the daughter of a Methodist bishop loomed large as well. Weary from his years of living alone, Baraq decided that love would conquer all the differences between the lovely Christian girl and the passionate Jewish boy. What he could not know, what young people in love never know, was that while he was certain that she was really a Jewish soul accidentally born into a Gentile body, she believed in her heart that Baraq would someday become a Christian.

Their marriage was unusual. Baraq insisted that his rabbi perform the actual ceremony, and Lyn's bishop father was invited to offer a prayer of consecration for the new couple. Both partners simply refused to think clearly about the religious and cultural differences that separated them. Lyn accepted a job as an elementary school teacher in Boston, and Baraq immersed himself in his studies at Brandeis University. Lyn attended church faithfully on Sunday, and Baraq agreed to help lead worship on Saturday at a small synagogue nearby. Their worlds began to revolve in different orbits.

The birth of a healthy son and a beautiful baby girl seemed to sanctify their union, and Baraq's academic career continued from one success to another. He discovered in Professor Gordon, who was everything Dr. Younger had promised, his true intellectual father. And Gordon returned Baraq's affection fully. Pushing Baraq to the limits of his capacity as a student, Gordon alternately prodded, chided, and encouraged his young follower to excel.

Sometimes, Baraq thought, Dr. Gordon had too much confidence in him. Noting to his mentor that he had been incorrectly enrolled in second year Egyptian hieroglyphs although he had not taken the first year, Baraq expected Gordon to approve a schedule change for him. But Gordon dismissed Baraq's concerns. "The only grade that counts will be the final examination at year's end. You will be behind the other students at first, but you are an experienced linguist. You'll catch up in time."

Baraq was not so sure. But he was determined to justify Gordon's faith in him. Although he later confessed, "I was lost for the first semester and one-half," Baraq somehow acquired the first-year material with which his classmates had begun the year, and he earned a "B" on the final. It was the only grade other than "A" that he ever received throughout twelve years in college and graduate school.

As had his master's thesis in Greek literature and his first doctoral dissertation at the seminary on Hebrew grammar, Baraq's second dissertation on Aramaic magic inscriptions marked him as a young scholar with a bright future.

A New Career, a New Crisis

When a major East Coast university created a new department of Judaic studies, Gordon's recommendation was crucial in helping Baraq win the job as their first professor. His future seemed secure. But his decision to accept a position teaching Judaism became the occasion for doubt to begin growing in the mind of his Methodist wife, who despaired of her husband's true intentions for the first time. As Baraq's career blossomed, Lyn slipped ever deeper into depression. She had not signed on to be the wife of a Jew but of a Christian biblical scholar. And Baraq seemed impervious to her feelings and her vision of their life together.

Most egregious of all for the monolingual Lyn, Baraq persisted in speaking only Hebrew to their young son David and their darling daughter Nicole. Not only was her husband Jewish, Lyn realized, but he was teaching their two children to be Jewish as well. The end was predictable, but the note Baraq found upon returning from class one afternoon was devastating. "I will always love you. But I am not the companion you need. And since the children are both more like their father than their mother, I have decided to leave them with you and return to the home of my parents. I wish you well."

To survive, Baraq immersed himself in his career. But as the single father of two small children, he had no choice except to drag his son and daughter with him everywhere he went—to class, to worship, to shop, to play. Students who applied to serve as Baraq's teaching assistant knew up front that part of the job was helping with the children. Whenever he received an invitation to offer a scholarly lecture or speak to a congregation out of town, Baraq's response was uniform: "I'll be happy to come, but you must agree to underwrite the travel expenses of my two children as well." Because their hectic schedule made public schooling impossible, Baraq became not only the father but also the private teacher of his two children.

Academically, Baraq flowered. Museums around the world hired him to decipher and publish a series of Aramaic inscriptions etched on various pieces of pottery in their collections, and each new publication added to his stature as an epigraphist. To this growing number of articles in scholarly journals, Baraq added impressive books and articles on the grammar of Hebrew, Aramaic, Babylonian cuneiform, and Egyptian hieroglyphics.

During his third year as a young professor, Mr. B died, and Baraq was called home to conduct the funeral. En route, Baraq realized that everyone present at the secular service would know that Mr. B had never been religious, shunned synagogue worship, and thought organized religion a waste of time. But Baraq was convinced that these facts did not define his grandfather. On the plane ride home, with only a Hebrew Bible and airline stationery in hand, Baraq wrote the remarks with which he would memorialize his grandfather. Yes, he would admit openly, Mr. B had not been "religious," and some might have judged him harshly as a result. But reaching beyond the boundaries of synagogue, prayer, and formal religious practice, Baraq turned to the great Hebrew prophet Micah, who had asked and answered what Baraq viewed as the quintessential question of life. "What does the Lord require?" Micah had asked. And Baraq affirmed that Mr. B had lived the heart of the prophetic answer: "To practice justice, to love faithfulness, and to live humbly with God."

After the service, Baraq was inundated with people who wanted to tell him of Mr. B's involvement in their lives. For the first time, he met people to whom his grandfather had lent money when they had no collateral but needed food and supplies, teachers and nurses from poor families whose tuition Mr. B had paid to allow them to attend college, and friends who remembered Mr. B as the one person who always stood by them in illness or despair. Their testimony confirmed to Baraq that he had assessed his grandfather correctly. Laying to rest the old man who had been his first hero and teacher, Baraq not only found solace for his own heart in the ancient words of Micah but defined for everyone present the essence of the man he had loved.

Shortly after returning to the university, Baraq received a plea from a small nearby synagogue whose rabbi had died suddenly and unexpectedly. Baraq accepted the offer to serve as their congregational rabbi on an interim basis, adding to his paternal and academic responsibilities the burden of spiritual leadership for a group of seventy-five families. Added to his academic responsibilities, *bar mitzvah* classes, adult education courses, hospital visits, family counseling, and services of prayer and worship filled his every waking moment.

Teaching young eleven and twelve-year old boys proved a particularly daunting task. Most were required to attend by insistent parents, and all would have preferred to spend their after-school hours at anything other than studying Hebrew with a rabbi. So, Baraq accepted the challenge of making classes interesting enough to hold the attention of wiggling pre-adolescents. During a vocabulary lesson, Baraq was determined to uncover a secret way to help the students remember difficult Hebrew words. Whenever he could, he linked the foreign words to familiar English ones. "The word for 'go up' in Hebrew is *nasa,* '" he noted, "just like the American space program."

But his plans came unraveled one afternoon. "The Hebrew word for 'tent' is *'ohel*," he explained, "just like the swear word." Reviewing later in the session, he called upon a particularly unruly boy to recall the Hebrew word for "tent," and when the boy's eyes rolled back in his head, Baraq reminded him of the earlier clue. "Remember, it's a swear."

Again, the eyes rolled, and there was a long pause. Finally, the beleaguered boy asked, "Is it *shit*?" The class roared, and Baraq gave silent thanks to God that most of his classes were conducted at the university level.

Even with his heavy schedule, Baraq remained devoted to his two children. Whenever little David or Nicole needed him to attend a school function, he was there. He served as an assistant coach for David's flag football team as well as for Nicole's volleyball squad. And his secretary was instructed that whenever Baraq scheduled something with his children, their appointments were to be honored as faithfully as if they had been made by an important congregant or professorial colleague. His attitude was obvious to David and little Nicole, as well as to everyone else in his life. They came first.

Still, Baraq needed help. He enrolled the children in public school and decided to hire a retired schoolteacher to tutor them and to stay with them until he could return from the tasks of his day. At home, Baraq was determined to be "Dad," not "rabbi" or "professor." His dedication to fatherhood resulted in the beginning of a lifelong friendship with David and Nicole. And in their presence, Baraq was free to be laugh, to hug, to cry, and often to be just plain silly. His sense of humor constantly delighted them, and their love sustained him.

To both children, Baraq bequeathed his ferocious spirit of independence; little David especially seemed to have inherited his father's sense of humor. One Halloween, the ten-year old boy squirted lighter fluid on his shoes and lit it, then ran through the neighborhood screaming that the devil had set his feet on fire. Learning from his father how to teach the family dog to "speak" with only a hand signal, David convinced his friends that the dog was a mathematical genius. "Ask him to tell you the sum of two plus two," David challenged his mates. Seeing his open hand, the dog began obediently to bark. When he reached the count of four, David slyly closed his hand into a fist, whereupon the dog immediately stopped. To the amazement of his friends, who never caught on to the trick, the clever dog gave one correct answer after another, no matter how they phrased the question.

Humor was one thing, but independence sometimes became a problem. Although David had been warned not to leave the backyard and enter the forested area behind the fence, Baraq returned early one afternoon to find his son missing. When he found him in the woods, Baraq issued a stern warning based upon his belief that physical punishment of a child was wrong: "The next time you go into the woods, it will cost you five dollars." And then, Baraq came home early again on the following day just to test his son. Once again, he was absent, and once again, he was located in the forbidden area. But before Baraq could speak, the young boy explained: "Dad, you said it would cost five dollars, so I left five bucks on your dresser before I came out here."

Baraq was not surprised to find the bill on his dresser exactly as described, but he wondered how the boy had concocted such a scheme. Sometimes, he thought ruefully, the apple does not fall far from the tree.

Nicole's independent streak also surfaced often. She cut her hair the way she liked it rather than in the style Baraq would have preferred. She refused to eat meat because "It tastes yucky." And then, during a ninth-grade civics class devoted to the topic of women in the military, Nicole boldly asserted that girls were just as tough as boys, and in the event of an attack on the nation, they should fight in combat units alongside the boys.

The teacher badly underestimated his young adversary. "Well, Nicole, how do you think your dad would feel if his little girl were to be killed in battle?"

The tiny beauty stamped her foot and snapped, "Exactly the same way he would feel if his little *boy* got shot!" When the teacher sent a note home complaining that Nicole had been disrespectful, Baraq listened to the story from his daughter and showed up at school with her on the following morning. "Hey," he told the startled teacher firmly, "when she's right, she's right."

Baraq's life was too full to allow time for self-pity—or a social life, specifically female companionship. He simply did not have time to date. To be sure, more than once, he was invited to a social gathering that featured several couples and a lone single lady, always conveniently seated next to Baraq at dinner. But Baraq seemed unaware of what his friends were anxious to accomplish. He was unfailingly polite and charming, yet he remained the rabbi, never the suitor.

For fifteen years, as parent, teacher, rabbi, and scholar, Baraq fulfilled the crushing obligations of the life he had chosen. And then, he crashed.

Meningitis and a New Start

The crash was as complete as it was unexpected. After he failed to arrive in class on time one morning, Baraq was found on the ground outside the building, eyes wide open but unable to speak or move. Meningitis! The fearful word that emerged after a battery of hospital tests was evidence to the hospital staff that Baraq was near the end of his life. He was transported back to Baton Rouge at the insistence of his mother, who now assumed responsibility for her only son and her two grandchildren. Miss Josephine, now a financially successful insurance executive, ordered that no expense be spared to save the life of her beloved boy. But several weeks elapsed with no change in Baraq's condition. He remained unable to speak.

Then, a young rabbi bounded into Baraq's hospital room like a curious puppy driven to discover everything possible about his new surroundings. Speaking Hebrew, he addressed Baraq. "Dr. Broulliette, I have read everything you have written, and I am thrilled to meet you. Just today, one of the nurses who belongs to our congregation told me you were here. She doesn't know who you are, just saw on the records that you are Jewish, and thought I should visit."

Because she did not speak Hebrew, Baraq's mom had no idea what the young rabbi was saying to her son. He seemed overly enthusiastic to her, but she did not fail to note that Baraq stirred slightly, apparently in an attempt to respond. It was the most encouraging sign in weeks.

The rabbi continued breathlessly, switching to English in deference to Miss Josephine. "I can't wait until you are well. You will attend service with us, you will accept an *'aliyah*, you will chant the Torah for our congregation, you will sing the *haftarah*, and you will become my tutor."

Baraq's mother was furious. How dare this stranger speak to her dying son that way, imposing upon him for his own benefit! If the young rabbi noticed, he gave no indication. But Miss Josephine watched in amazement and then gratitude as her son, for the first time since the crash, began to speak slowly.

"I hope you won't be disappointed, but I don't think I will be able to attend services again. But thank you for the invitation and the kind words."

Even Baraq's negative response did nothing to dull the enthusiasm of the energetic rabbi. "Of course, it will take time. But I know that you will soon be well, and then, you will join us." With that, the young rabbi spread his hands over Baraq's head and prayed. "May the One who blessed Abraham, Isaac, and Jacob now bless you with complete healing of body and spirit. Amen." Planting a tender kiss on Baraq's cheek, he swept out of the room as rambunctiously as he had entered. He returned almost every day for the following three months.

According to the later testimony of Baraq, it was the sheer energy and unbounded optimism of Rabbi Green that had given him the will to recover. Soon, he left the hospital, still weak but able to walk short distances on his own. And Rabbi Green began a routine of twice-weekly visits to Baraq's home. The two men studied, prayed, and discussed subjects ranging from sports to politics.

As Baraq grew stronger, the young rabbi discovered his delicious sense of humor. With a roasted chicken on the table between them at lunchtime, the rabbi asked Baraq to offer a blessing. Expecting the familiar "Blessed are You, O God, King of the universe, who brings forth food from the ground," Rabbi Green was startled by a version he had never heard before delivered with a straight face in flawless Hebrew: "Blessed are you, O God, King of the universe, who brings forth *chicken from the oven*." Baraq did not even smile, but the young rabbi collapsed in a paroxysm of laughter. It was a side of Baraq few people had ever seen.

But in every meeting, Rabbi Green never failed to remind Baraq that he expected to see him in the synagogue sooner rather than later. As Baraq's birthday approached, plans were made for him to attend service for the first time with Rabbi Green—and to sing the *haftarah* portion of the morning.

On the Saturday morning of his fiftieth birthday, Baraq arrived at the synagogue, where about one hundred worshipers had gathered. Because they had heard so much about him from Rabbi Green, they greeted Dr. Broulliette as an old friend rather than as a stranger worshiping with them for the first time. When it was time for the *haftarah,* two young men had to help Baraq climb the three steps up to the *bimah*, and the congregation, assured by the rabbi that their feeble visitor was a great scholar in their midst, waited nervously.

Slowly, Baraq began to sing the *haftarah*, the prophetic passage of the Bible chosen to augment the Torah reading for the week. At first, his voice was barely a whisper, but the words he sang seemed to infuse him with strength. "Comfort, comfort my people, says our God. Speak to the heart of Jerusalem and call out to her that her difficult service has ended, that she has received from the hand of the Lord double for all her transgressions." Baraq's voice regained full force as he reached the words "Lift up your voice with strength," and his powerful bass filled the sanctuary.

When Baraq finished, he was completely spent but triumphant. Helped from the *bimah*, every congregant wanted to touch him and congratulate him in the traditional Hebrew fashion: *Yasher koach*, "Well done." Tears of joy coursed down Baraq's cheeks as he embraced his new friends. He felt that he had been reborn.

The succeeding days brought regular small steps of improvement in Baraq's health. Less than four months later, he was strong enough to attend services regularly, to chant the Torah portion and its *haftarah*, and to lead the congregation in traditional prayers of worship and praise.

Just as he felt his strength returning, his mother died, and once again, Baraq was called upon by the family to speak at her funeral. As he had when confronted with the challenge of honoring his grandfather, again Baraq turned to the Hebrew Scriptures. This time, his theme was designed to answer the question of Proverbs: "Who can find a virtuous woman?" Describing his mother as the embodiment of the biblical heroine, Baraq sketched her life of care for her family, her strength in the face of adversity, and her unwavering faith in her son. When Baraq cited the verse promising that the children of such a woman would surely "stand and call her blessed," no one present doubted that he had offered her the ultimate tribute.

Back in the Classroom

Baraq was now a regular at synagogue services. The congregation at one service in the spring of that year included a visitor from LSU, the Presbyterian professor of Old Testament who before that time had been unaware of Baraq's presence in Baton Rouge but who became convinced that Baraq would make a worthy addition to the university faculty of religious studies. Through his insistence, the dean was persuaded to offer Baraq a teaching position in the department of religion. Able to teach only part-time at first, Baraq gradually increased his schedule to full-time over the following three years and slowly resumed the career that he had assumed his bout with meningitis had ended forever.

But even before his first class, a fascinating minidrama occurred with Rabbi Green. During one of their regular study sessions together, Baraq had effortlessly explained a difficult passage of Scripture to his young partner. When the rabbi professed to be dazzled by the brilliance of the interpretation, Baraq insisted that it was really nothing new or unknown to scholars. Convinced that Baraq's interpretation was unique, the young rabbi asked him to write the explanation for him to study more in depth. Without Baraq's knowledge, he typed Baraq's handwritten paper and submitted it to a prominent scholarly journal. When the letter accepting the article for publication arrived, Rabbi Green offered it as proof to Baraq that his scholarly career was far from ended, despite his two-year absence from teaching. This incident emboldened Baraq to begin once again to participate in scholarly debates about the significant issues of the day, and as he restarted his teaching career at LSU, he also began once again to produce a flood of scholarly writings.

His personal life was a different story. He was finally strong enough to welcome his two children back into the home that he purchased near the campus, and the family began picking up the pieces of their life. Young David was now grown, and shortly after the move, entered military service to become a tank commander in the US Army Corps of Combat Engineers. But Nicole was entering the difficult teen years without a mother. Remembering his own struggles with only a single parent, saddened by the fact that Lyn had lost contact with her daughter, Baraq became open to the possibility of finding a mate for himself who would also provide Nicole a surrogate mother. A young Catholic lady studying for conversion to Judaism caught his eye, but it was her two-month-old baby girl who captured his heart. Intent on providing a father for the infant Abigail and a mother for Nicole, Baraq ignored the twenty-year age difference between the baby's mother and himself, married the young convert, and legally adopted her infant daughter.

This relationship, like his first two loves, was destined to end badly. Within a year, his new wife abandoned both her own child and Baraq, moving to a distant state. Instead of finding a mother for Nicole, Baraq had merely acquired a second daughter for whom he was responsible. As the father of two motherless daughters whom he had to rear on his own, he did what he had done before, embracing his children and the task of parenting them, hurling himself into his academic career, and finding spiritual solace in the synagogue.

Alone Again

Day followed day as Baraq settled once again into a routine with which he was all too familiar. Sixteen-year old Nicole bonded with the new baby and cared for her more like a mother than a sister. Baraq taught, wrote, spoke often at scholarly conferences and interfaith gatherings, and fell into an exhausted sleep night after night. The two girls and their father forged a family unit that brought Baraq warmth, love, and comfort. But again, there was simply no time to think about his own loneliness. There would be no more loves for him, Baraq decided. The fear of abandonment overwhelmed any thought he might have entertained about finding lasting happiness with another partner.

Once a Rabbi, Always a Rabbi

Once again, a small congregation came calling. Located 125 miles from Baton Rouge, sixty-five Jewish families in Lake Charles struggled to maintain their distinctive traditions and lifestyle. Unable for years to afford a full-time rabbi, they had witnessed a succession of young rabbinical students or elderly retired rabbis trundle in and out once or twice each month, holding services but seldom finding time for other rabbinical duties—counseling, visitation of the sick, continuing education, etc. Initially, Baraq was invited to spend a single weekend with the tiny congregation, presenting several lectures about the traditions of Judaism. A mutual love affair blossomed. As much as they needed stable spiritual leadership, Baraq needed a spiritual family. Soon, he was driving regularly to Lake Charles twice each month, serving them as rabbi and finding in them the Jewish family that he needed.

As it had done once before, Baraq's exhausting schedule proved almost fatal. This time, instead of being found unconscious on a university campus, a dog that had not quite finished her training gave Baraq the warning that saved his life. That dog, of course, was Lilit, whose story I had learned in my first Google search about Dr. Broulliette.

Although she was the star of the drama, Lilit was far from the only significant player in this latest health crisis that visited Baraq. Because of his weakened condition following the heart attack, Baraq was preparing to sever his ties to the Lake Charles congregation when he was approached by a student serving as his teaching assistant. Derek was a former linebacker who had wrecked a knee and any hope of a pro career while making a tackle against LSU's chief football rival, Ole Miss. His interest in languages had led him to Hebrew classes taught by Dr. Broulliette, and the two had become friends. As a kinesiology major, Derek was convinced that he could help Dr. Broulliette recover from the debilitating effects of his heart attack.

Seated in the office of his professor, Derek offered two propositions. "I can drive you to Lake Charles, and I can establish a routine of physical therapy that will get you back in good condition." Thereafter, Dr. Broulliette and Derek, the 175-pound professor and the 260-pound ex-linebacker, taught, traveled, and exercised together. And Derek was correct. Slowly, Dr. Broulliette began to regain his strength. After three months on the program designed for him by Derek, Dr. Broulliette was able to walk, carry his own briefcase, climb stairs, and resume a normal schedule. His restored physical condition also allowed him to increase the frequency of his trips to serve the Lake Charles congregation.

Baraq's home life also changed. Nicole, now an LSU graduate, married, gave him a grandson and embarked on a career of her own, leaving Baraq to share his home with only his adopted daughter, Lilit, and a succession of abused or abandoned dogs taken in for rescue, training, and placement with loving families.

David was now twenty-eight and retired from the army. He took a job a thousand miles away but called often and visited when he could. He would always be Baraq's best friend. Nicole also moved far away, but she, too, stayed in close contact with her father. At home in Baton Rouge, his adopted daughter Abigail was the light of Baraq's life, and she proved invaluable to him by caring for the dogs on weekends that required Baraq's presence in Lake Charles. But he could not shake the feeling that he was unable to connect with her as he had with his two older children.

The dissolution of Nicole's marriage brought Baraq the usual feelings a father has when his daughter has been ill-treated but also produced a salutary effect as well. After two years as a single mother, Nicole entered the world of internet dating and began to regale her father with stories of how easy it was to meet people in this modern, twenty-first-century mode. Never believing for a moment that he would actually find a suitable mate for life, hoping only to find a conversation partner, a friend, Baraq finally succumbed to the urging of Nicole, sending a photo and a short description of himself to a popular internet dating service.

The results were about what he had expected. To be sure, he exchanged numerous e-mail messages with female subscribers, even spoke with some of them by telephone. Once, he even met an attractive Jewish lady living in New Orleans, but he could not bring himself to call for a second date. "The old *buzzeroo* was just not there," he explained to Nicole by phone.

The most intriguing contact he made was with an oncologist living in Connecticut, with whom he enjoyed several lengthy and engaging conversations. But the distance between them and his hectic schedule set to rest any idea he might have entertained of a meeting in person. "Besides," he protested, "who would want a beat-up old scudder like me!"

Baraq told himself repeatedly that "One is a good number." He had his beautiful daughter and his faithful dog for companionship, his teaching and research for intellectual stimulation, and his loyal congregation for spiritual depth. His nights were still lonely, but he gave himself no time for self-pity. "Marriage is a wonderful institution," he explained to a well-meaning friend, "but I'm still too young to be institutionalized."

Still, no matter how hard he tried, Baraq could not escape the blunt statement of the Torah found in the second chapter of Genesis: "It is *not* good for a man to be alone."

The Widow

I watched the elegant lady coming out of the funeral home, then opened her door as she reached the car I was driving for her. Sixty years had not masked her beauty, and grief had bowed her shoulders only slightly. The smile remained, less radiant but still there. "Let's go home, Carlita," she spoke distinctly, though softer than usual.

This was her second funeral in less than one month. Three weeks earlier, her beloved husband of twenty-five years had finally succumbed to cancer, and now she was burying the mother for whom she had cared faithfully during the long and difficult months that inevitably accompany the ravages of Alzheimer's.

For ten years, I had been Miss Sara's constant companion: driver, cook, housekeeper, nurse, personal assistant, and friend. Her wisdom and care for me through my own health crisis had not only saved my life; they had given me an unbounded admiration for her. Problems that seemed insurmountable to me were for her merely opportunities to exhibit grit and determination until the solution, which she always discovered, was reached. She was the sweetest but also the strongest person, male or female, I had ever met. Now, seeing for the first time a vein of vulnerability threading through her persona, I realized that I truly did not know her at all.

Oh, I knew that we could not have been more different. She was an American Jew; I was a Mexican Catholic. She had earned both an M.A. in journalism and an M.S. in computer technology; I had left high school a year short of graduation. She was childless; I had become a mother at age seventeen. To me, although she lived modestly, she seemed quite wealthy, while both my husband and I worked just to provide for our family of five. Beyond that, I really did not know who she was or what made her tick.

Grief was soon to provide the window that allowed me to look deep into the soul of my remarkable employer, a window that opened for the first time on the morning after her mom's funeral. Entering her room, expecting to find her dressed as usual, drinking her second cup of strong coffee, and reading the newspaper, I found her still asleep. She stirred when I opened her door and sat up slowly, revealing swollen eyes that had obviously wept well into the night. The ubiquitous smile was tinged with sadness. Her "good morning" was welcoming yet softer than normal, and I sensed that she wanted me to stay with her for a moment or two.

"I don't know what to do now," she began. "I've been alone before, when I was much younger, but this is different somehow." That morning and countless mornings to follow prompted her to pour out the story of her life to me. At home each evening, I began to compile a notebook of our conversations, writing in my native Spanish. What follows is the English version of those notes that my son's LSU friend Jeff helped me polish.

The Early Years

The year was 1947. Boston was windy and cold in April, but the appearance of their first child brought warmth and cheer to Jacob and Elizabeth Meyers. In accordance with Jewish tradition, the name of the baby girl was chosen in remembrance of her maternal great-grandmother, Sara. She was a beautiful child, of course, as are all baby girls. But it was quickly apparent that she was anything but a delicate flower of femininity. Even as an infant, whenever she crawled, her shoulders tilted slightly forward, aimed at the target she was attempting to reach.

When she was only three months old, her parents moved with her to the small town of Alexandria, Louisiana, home to a modest community of about thirty Jewish families, including Sara's paternal grandparents and two uncles and their wives. Baby Sara soon became the favorite companion of her father, and he was seldom seen without her trotting along at his side. But as much as she delighted her father, Sara seemed equally to frustrate her mother. Elizabeth had come from a prosperous family, and Jacob proved incapable of providing for her materially in the way to which she was accustomed and to which she felt entitled. She often voiced the opinion that the countless hours Jacob wasted spoiling his daughter would be better spent trying to find a better job or at least earn a promotion from his current employer that would increase the family income. In addition, every time Jacob praised his daughter, Elizabeth interpreted it as a silent rebuke of her. Sara was beautiful. Elizabeth knew that her looks were quite ordinary. Sara was funny. Elizabeth was a notorious grouch. Sara loved Jewish holidays. Elizabeth viewed them as little more than additional work for her. Sara soon learned that "Mama" was never pleased with "Dad"—or with her.

Part of the problem stemmed from the fact that Sara was often ill. Her chest ached; her legs cramped; she sweltered in the Louisiana heat. It seemed to Elizabeth that her life as a mother was spent nursing a sickly child, while Jacob plodded along, content with his job and reveling in time shared with Sara. Once Sara grasped the fact that her mother was not happy with her, she became shy and withdrawn, preferring to play alone rather than "pester" her beleaguered mom. When she began school, books became her best friends, and her alone time allowed her to escape the constant criticism of her mother. She became a fixture at the small local library, and the librarian once remarked that Sara surely must have read every book on the shelves at least twice.

One morning, during the summer following her fifth-grade school year, Sara marched up to the checkout desk with four bulky volumes in hand. The young assistant on desk duty did not know the tiny girl and saw only an eleven-year-old child who could not possibly understand the books she was trying to check out: "These books are for big people," she noted firmly. "You should read books for people your own age."

Fortunately, the senior librarian, who knew Sara well, intervened with a reassuring wink at the young reader. "Oh, this is Sara," she explained to the assistant. "She can check out anything she wants."

Except for her battles with illness and the touchy relationship with her mother, Sara was happy during those first twelve years of her life in Alexandria. The fifties preceded computers, cell phones, and other electronic gadgets without which modern young people so quickly became unable to exist. But exciting children's games could be created on demand by the Meyers clan, which had quickly grown to include Sara's younger brother Isaac and five cousins: mock play acting, doctor and nurse, hide-and-go-seek, dressing like grown-ups, kick the can ... and baseball.

Baseball was still America's game in those days, and Sara's dad had been a promising shortstop in the minor league system of the St. Louis Cardinals until a freak injury had wrecked his powerful arm. But the injury that had cost him his own shot at stardom could not dull his ardor for his beloved sport, and when he played with the children, as he did often, baseball was always the game of choice.

Because of her dad, the Cardinals became Sara's favorite team, and Stan Musial was her first hero. She decided as a small girl that she would one day play shortstop for the Cardinals, often drifting off to sleep with visions of making a perfect throw to "Stan the Man" at first just in time to nip a speedy runner. No one bothered to explain to her that girls could not play baseball, so she just played the game. Her athletic ability was obvious—an easy way of scooping up hot ground balls, an accurate throw to first that regularly beat the runner, even a short, compact swing of the bat that sent line drives over the heads of infielders. Sara was a natural. When the normally placid Jacob threatened to sue the city unless his daughter was allowed to join a Little League team, baseball became the opportunity for Sara to shed her shyness.

In addition to being a natural athlete, Sara was far and away the most competitive player on the field. Jacob had the infinite patience required to teach the game to children, but Sara did not. Dad would not fuss at an infielder for booting a ground ball, but Sara did not hesitate. And woe to the player who failed to run hard to first even on a routine fly ball. Sara wanted to win, and she pushed not only herself but her teammates mercilessly.

Maybe it was her love for baseball, maybe it was her willingness to play catch until dark every evening, or maybe it was just the normal bond that develops naturally between a father and a daughter. But everyone, not just Elizabeth, knew that Sara and Jacob had a "thing" together. His humor first brought to her face the smile that thereafter never seemed to leave. His steely arms comforted her when a bad hop ground ball bloodied her lip. His unquestioned devotion convinced her that she was worth loving. And his unwavering confidence in her told her that there was nothing she could not accomplish.

Sara's toughness was matched by another personality characteristic that would define her entire life. Whenever baby brother Isaac or a younger cousin cried, it was Sara who came to the rescue, becoming virtually a surrogate parent to the six younger children. When a wounded or abandoned animal whimpered, it was Sara who cared for it. "Dad, we have to adopt this puppy" became an oft-repeated phrase, and Jacob often relented, turning a deaf ear to the objections of Elizabeth.

Sara's grandmother provided the Jewish flavor for the extended family. Friday evening candles brightening the Shabbat dinner table, special costumes for Purim, exotic ethnic foods, and especially the annual Passover celebration with thirty relatives were an integral component of Sara's view of herself and her world.

Jewish holidays and other special family occasions received a boost when Elizabeth convinced Jacob to quit his sales job and open a small restaurant. Birthdays, school honors, anniversaries, and holidays regularly featured the entire family at the restaurant. Sara came to love these times, and she developed a strong sense of her own identity within the family. She was Jewish, of course. Wasn't everybody!

But Jacob was not a wise businessman, and the restaurant failed when Sara was only fourteen. When Jacob could not find work in tiny Alexandria, he was forced to accept a job in New Orleans. It was Sara who missed him the most. When a playmate horrified Sara with the hint that her father and mother were heading for divorce, Jacob dutifully began making the four-hour round trip from New Orleans every weekend in an effort to reassure his beloved daughter. Nothing would come between the father and his baby girl. And when the family decided to move to New Orleans for her father's job, Sara's focus was not on the loss of the familiar or the friends she was leaving but on the chance to spend more time with Dad.

The Big City

The move from Alexandria to the big city was difficult. Because they lived in a predominantly Jewish area of the city, most of Sara's classmates were Jewish. But the small-town girl had never before witnessed what seemed to her to be an attitude of disrespect for teachers and other adults. Flying erasers and talking out loud were unknown in Alexandria classrooms, as were "cheeky" responses to and arguments with teachers. But the kids in New Orleans were unruly and often mean-spirited. Sara, her smile never absent, was "different," small-town polite, and once again shy. Her teachers loved her, but fellow students viewed her as an outsider.

When Sara was in the ninth grade, an incident during Halloween in the new city made things worse. Next door to the Meyers family lived Wally, the star running back for the local high school that Sara was slated to attend the following year. With no malice, just the faulty judgment of an immature teen, he decided to play a trick on the children. Dressed in an outrageous costume and wearing a frightful mask, he hid behind a clump of bushes and jumped directly in front of Sara and her ten-year old brother as they returned from a pickup baseball game. Isaac froze in terror, but Sara did not hesitate. She attacked with her trusty bat, landing a solid blow to the right side of the older boy's shin that shattered the bone. Jacob, just returning from work, jumped from his car barely in time to keep Sara from taking a second powerful swing at the now prostrate "demon," this time aiming at his head!

The running back's leg was fractured, and his season was over. Even worse, with his demise, the team had no chance of success in the state playoffs. In football-crazed Louisiana, such a prospect was considered a tragedy of major proportions. But Sara explained hotly that she thought her little brother was going to be hurt, and she refused to apologize. "Apologize? Never! If another demon attacks Isaac, I'll do it again."

Neither Wally's parents nor the coach, who was furious with his star player for his terrible judgment, blamed Sara—nor did the injured footballer. But Wally had a younger sister in Sara's class, and she made certain that everyone knew who had incapacitated her big brother. Sara made few friends in school after that, and she retreated once more to the cocoon of books.

Still, New Orleans was not all negative. Sara was enrolled in classes at a local synagogue and soon proved an apt and willing student who eagerly grasped the rudiments of the Hebrew language and the basic elements of Jewish history and tradition. She looked forward to the simple Friday evening prayer service with her family and believed the rabbi was speaking directly to her with the words that ended each service: "May the Lord bless and guard you. May the Lord shine His face in your direction and be gracious to you. May the Lord lift up His face toward you and grant you *Shalom*." Reform Jews did not do the *bar* or *bat mitzvah* thing in those days, but Sara was an active member of the special confirmation class honored by the congregation during her junior year in high school. She loved being Jewish and never imagined any other way of life.

Because the meager income of her father required every family member to contribute financially, Elizabeth took a clerical job in a local business, and Sara found occasional work as a babysitter with families that lived nearby. She also accepted with grace the dresses sent from Alexandria by her wealthier aunts when they had tired of wearing them. To make the dresses fit her properly, Sara learned to sew, first for herself and then for other family members as well. Although she never felt poor, Sara was not unaware of the fact that most of the big city kids her age possessed more material things than her. Dad, books, and her rabbi combined to give her a strong sense of self-worth, and her steps into self-reliance were measured and firm. She learned to ignore the frequent criticisms of Elizabeth as well as the gnawing pain that persisted in bedeviling her body, surfacing routinely in the form of leg cramps that made walking difficult and rendered running impossible.

As she matured and her body morphed from little girl to young woman, Sara's athletic activities were pushed to the background, crowded out by parties and boys. Her beauty attracted the opposite sex like a magnet, and her dating calendar was always full. But even with a busy social calendar, Sara continued to work outside the home, sitting with smaller children, running errands for busy working mothers, or sewing dresses that other girls could wear on special occasions.

And she excelled as a student. While others struggled to earn high marks, Sara proved capable of grasping easily whatever subjects came her way. Her extensive reading and her natural curiosity served her well, and she graduated from high school at the top of her class. College was the logical and unquestioned next step.

College Life, Work, and First Love

Undergraduate life brought yet another shift in Sara's perspective on her social world. Still, there was abundant male companionship, now accompanied by parties at which alcohol and marijuana were omnipresent. It was the sixties, after all. And though she drank only moderately and sampled marijuana only sporadically, sometimes even inhaling (!), Sara remained in the center of a whirl of social activity. But because the boys her own age were less mature than she was, Sara never became seriously involved with only one special dating partner. Fun was the goal, not a serious relationship.

Grades continued to come easily to the young party girl, but she never really understood why schoolwork was important. Many freshman classes at Louisiana State University were little more than an exercise in numbers; some of Sara's classes met in a huge auditorium that could seat hundreds of students. Freshman and sophomore students in such courses rarely saw professors. They merely sat in front of giant TV screens listening to recorded lectures. Once each week, a graduate assistant would appear to collect papers and announce additional assignments, but the atmosphere was cold and impersonal, and actual learning occurred only if an individual student furnished his or her own motivation. Tests were little more than exercises in memorization and regurgitation, requiring little creative or independent thought. In addition, because there were few Jewish students at LSU, Sara began to mingle with non-Jews as her social skills grew.

After only three semesters of these cattle-call classes, bored with immature college boys and frustrated at her lack of spendable income, Sara decided that college was a waste of her time and dropped out to enter the real world of work. She quickly found employment as a secretary, mastering her new tasks as easily as she had conquered schoolwork. But her new companions at work were older, most were married, and Sara could not relate to them well. Worst of all, Sara noticed that the other women in the office had no thoughts of anything beyond a simple clerical position. Life settled into a repetitious cycle, encompassing little more than her humdrum job and an occasional meaningless date. She often dreamed of advancement, of more meaningful responsibility, of making a difference, only to learn that her suggestions were not welcomed by her supervisor. She retreated once again to shyness and books, going out after work only once or twice each month. Of greatest importance to Sara was the fact that she was independent, earning her own money, paying her own way, making her own decisions.

Two years into her career as a secretary, Sara met a handsome young man who swept her off her feet. He was not Jewish, but Sara had drifted away from her own upbringing and had come to think of religious faith rarely if at all. Since Stuart had been reared in a secular home, both he and Sara sincerely believed their relationship could succeed. In fact, they both considered their union to be "non-faith" rather than "interfaith." They married quickly in a civil ceremony and moved shortly after the wedding to Nashville, where Stuart had been hired as a salesman for a beer distributorship.

For the second time in her life, Sara and her father were separated by distance that denied them the chance to spend quality time together. She had traded a large extended family for a small cellular unit of two. The distance lengthened when the second marital year was spent in Los Angeles, and Sara was unable to see Jacob during the entire fifteen months. The third year brought the young couple to Memphis, where Stuart embarked on a career as a management trainee for an air freight company. The new position demanded frequent out-of-town trips, and Sara saw Stuart less and less. She continued to read, continued to work as a secretary, and began to spend long evenings alone.

The marriage began to falter as a result of Sara's loneliness and Stuart's "problem." On the road, Stuart preferred to drink with customers or fellow workers and seldom returned to his motel room early enough to telephone Sara. Sara continued to suffer the ache of loneliness. Worse still, the pains in her legs began to extend to her chest and seldom went away. Her confidence faltered, and she began to wonder what she had done to disappoint Stuart. Was it her inability to bear a child? Was she simply no longer attractive in his eyes? Had Stuart found another woman? But even as such thoughts came, Sara was forced to admit to herself that Stuart was not the man she had imagined *him* to be. Her feelings for him faded, and she began to think about an exit strategy. More than once she lay in bed alone, knowing that Stuart was engaged in another bout of heavy drinking somewhere, while thoughts of the possibility that he might die in a tragic accident—or that he simply might not come home this time—danced uninvited through her mind.

When Stuart was promoted and relieved of the frequent sales trips that had sent him out of the city, Sara decided to give the relationship one more chance. Rushing home from work on the afternoon of her husband's first day as a manager, Sara prepared Stuart's favorite meal of brisket, roast potatoes and carrots, cheese apples, and a delicious chocolate mousse. Minutes passed, and then hours, before Stuart finally stumbled home too drunk to eat. After weeks of the same routine, Sara realized that nothing had changed. Stuart still preferred his colleagues, and the bottle, to her. Thoughts of a possible exit resurfaced.

It was in Memphis that the chest pains could no longer be ignored, but Sara was reluctant to seek medical treatment. Because her mother and other family members had chosen to define her constant aches as little more than growing pains or jangled nerves, Sara had always refused to feel sorry for herself and had seldom complained. In Memphis, after years of chronic pain, Sara was finally forced to admit that she needed help, and she agreed to see a physician. A battery of tests revealed the problem to be a faulty heart valve that inadequately controlled the flow of blood to her extremities. Finally, there was an explanation for her aching legs and chest, but the explanation came with a shock. Surgery would be required.

Since Stuart's health insurance did not cover major surgery, Sara vowed to return to her normal life. She tried to rest more frequently, and she tried unsuccessfully to wean herself from smoking. She was young; she would be strong. She had lived with a faulty valve for twenty-six years. Surely, she could survive for the time needed to save enough money for surgery.

But her body betrayed her. She collapsed at work and was rushed to an emergency room, where doctors confirmed that she had suffered a minor heart attack and insisted that immediate surgery was required. What should have been a simple procedure turned into a four-hour attempt to save her life. The valve could not be repaired and had to be replaced with an artificial one. The only good news was that prompt action by the emergency room surgeon had minimized the long- term damage to her heart. Months of slow recovery were made tolerable only by the prospect of finally living a normal life as a wife—and perhaps even as a mother.

But the ordeal changed Stuart more than it did Sara. He resented the fact that Sara's surgery had plunged them into debt, and he spent even less time with her. Their conversations were rare and brief, physical intimacy ceased, and even when both were home at the same time, they were not actually together. Sara blamed herself for the difficulties, and she tried everything she knew to make the relationship work. But Stuart did not like her cooking, had no interest in the numerous books she was reading, and cared nothing about her progress on the job. They no longer lived together; they merely occupied the same apartment.

The result was inevitable, and Stuart finally expressed his true feelings late one evening. "I don't think any man could find you attractive now" was his fumbling explanation to the frail woman still weeks away from full recovery, and the marriage came to a crashing end.

The Working Girl and College Part Two

Sara was surprised that her reaction was more relief than sadness. Her "family" had dipped from two to one, but she knew that "one is a good number," if the one is someone to be trusted. And Sara decided to trust herself. Determined to succeed in the world of business, she plunged into her work, only to learn that her lack of a college degree limited her opportunities for advancement.

"Perhaps I am no longer attractive," she told her father while declining his invitation to move back home to New Orleans, "but I am still tough enough to do whatever it takes to live, not just somehow but triumphantly." Her shoulders hunched a bit more forward, Sara moved to Baton Rouge alone, found a tiny apartment near the campus, enrolled in college again, and continued part-time secretarial work with an airline to pay her own way. Her airline employee status allowed her to travel extensively on weekends, and she never indulged in self-pity or stopped to catch her breath.

Her second college experience was nothing like the first. The high grades continued, but now she studied resolutely and with a purpose. Parties and male companionship became distant memories as Sara focused on preparing herself to succeed in the world of business. A senior year course in statistics, required for a business degree, was almost her undoing. But the professor, who ran his own small consulting company in addition to his teaching assignment, came to her rescue. He recognized not only her talent and ability but especially her drive and will to succeed. After class one afternoon, he offered to tutor her, and Sara, struggling for the first time in her college career, quickly accepted. Her grade climbed, and her confidence grew.

The professor was everything Stuart had not been. He shared her love of reading, complimented her efforts, and seemed genuinely interested in her as a person, not just a student. Soon the professor and the student were spending long hours together and enjoying activities that had nothing to do with tutoring. Sara fought her feelings of affection for the professor, assuming that she was being silly. He was twenty years older than she was, and Sara laughed at some of the thoughts that entered her head.

But the professor had ideas of his own, and he shocked her with an invitation to spend the weekend with him at his small ranch. Sara accepted both his invitation and his amorous advances and returned to campus feeling giddy, alive, and special. A graduate assistant brought her crashing back to earth by informing her casually, "I know how you feel. The ranch is a cool place." Noting Sara's look of surprise, she added, "Oh, I was the professor's tutorial project last year."

Sick at her own foolish act, Sara refused the professor's offers of additional tutoring and through sheer grit earned a solid "B" in the course, her only grade other than "A" in four years of classes. It would be a long time before she would trust a male again. She did not need to be anyone's "girl," certainly did not need someone to take care of her, and she renewed her belief in the "one is a good number" mantra.

Summa cum laude graduation with a major in business and finance provided a job offer commensurate with her talents. Her new position as the business manager with a trucking company in New Orleans brought her into an apartment close to Dad, paid well, and allowed ample free time for travel and exploration.

But Stuart had been wrong. Sara was still attractive. Her heart problem solved, her smile still radiant, Sara seldom lacked male companionship. Her experiences with Stuart and the professor had made her too cautious to allow anything close to a long-term commitment, but life was once again joyous. Sara had an adequate income, time for travel and leisure, a future. And on several of her weekend jaunts, she was accompanied by the number-one man in her life, Dad.

Without realizing what was happening, Sara had continued to undergo another important transformation. The young woman who had grown up as the quintessential Jewish girl now lived and worked in a Christian environment. Virtually all her colleagues and friends were Christian, few of them were religiously observant, and most were unaware of Sara's religious heritage. Sara was never ashamed or secretive about her Jewishness; she simply found no compelling reason to remain active in the world of Judaism. Synagogue services and observance of Jewish holidays receded into the background of the new and thoroughly modern young businesswoman.

Michael

Sara advanced rapidly with her new company. To enhance her writing skills, she earned a master's degree in journalism at Tulane University. On her thirtieth birthday, she was promoted to the position of senior manager of the company's national offices, a change that would require her to move to the home office in Chicago. With two weeks of vacation time due before her move, Sara paid for her parents to accompany her on a vacation in Florida. Assuming that she and her dad would have little time together once she was in Chicago, Sara was determined to devote the entire time to him.

Her plans changed dramatically on the second night, when she was asked to dance by a man she had met briefly earlier that afternoon during a stroll with Jacob on the beach. Fifteen years her senior, confident and athletic, Michael was recovering from his own painful divorce that had left him skeptical and cautious. When he asked Sara and her parents to join him for dinner, Sara was amazed at the ease with which Michael charmed her mother. Elizabeth seemed to hang on Michael's every word and even laughed at his jokes, and Sara knew that he was an unusual man indeed.

But Sara's mom was not the only lady whom Michael charmed. His attraction to Sara was obvious, and Sara found herself enjoying the attention without taking it overly seriously. When she learned that Michael was working in Chicago, her heart fluttered, but she dismissed as a long shot the idea that they might see each other in her new city, the kind of thing that never really worked out. Instead, she decided simply to enjoy a few days of relaxation with a courteous and interesting companion whom she would probably never see when she left Florida.

For the next several days, Sara and Michael were an item. They swam, went on a day cruise, ate together, and talked long hours with each other, revealing secrets neither one shared readily, especially about their failed marriages. But Michael told Sara about more than his past. He shared with her his vision for a future of success in the corporate world, and Sara never doubted that he would accomplish his goals.

On his last night in Florida, two days before Sara's vacation ended, Michael seemed unduly anxious, and Sara finally blurted out an anguished "What's wrong?" before she could stop herself.

Michael's face became pale, and he spoke in quiet and measured tones. "When you and I are together, Sara, I find myself thinking something that I thought was impossible. I want to give love a second chance."

"Love?" Sara, too, had thought such an idea impossible for her.

"Yes, Sara, love. I think I am falling in love with you and would like to see where our relationship might go if we gave it a chance. Please say that we can continue seeing each other in Chicago."

Sara remained silent for several moments, and Michael feared that he had stepped out of bounds. Sara's measured response reassured him. "Okay, Michael. I'm willing to see what happens." Then, she added a proviso. "But I have grown comfortable taking care of myself, and I cannot relinquish my independence."

Like her first husband, Michael was not Jewish. Unlike Stuart, however, he was not threatened by Sara's intellect and strength. A former college athlete and Navy officer, Michael was on the fast track in the corporate world, and some of his colleagues assumed that the beautiful, younger Sara was little more than his "trophy"; only Michael and Sara understood the true nature of their interdependence and respect for one another. He shared with her his knowledge of business and became her mentor about money matters, helping her to dream of her own future as a financially independent woman. She became the love of his life.

But Michael was not all business, and he and Sara began to share times of enrichment and fun: concerts, museums, and books. Michael loved to read as much as Sara did, and they often shared the same book, discussing it during lazy Sunday afternoons before enjoying dinner together. Michael was also a huge sports fan who knew almost as much about baseball as Sara did. But because "fan" is merely the shortened form of "fanatic," they encountered the first potential roadblock to their friendship during their first fall together, when LSU played Florida in football. Michael had been a track star at Florida, and he loved Gator football as only a true fan[atic] can, while Sara had grown up dancing to the strains of "Hold That Tiger." Trying to watch the first half of the game together was a disaster. At halftime, they agreed that two things had to happen if they were to keep from strangling each other. Sara had to return to her own apartment for the second half, and they had to agree never, ever, to discuss the game regardless of the winner. When LSU finally beat Florida that afternoon, ending a three-year losing skein, Sara was true to her promise and said not a word. Michael, too, kept his promise and silently reassured himself that next year, Florida would return to its winning ways.

That winter, Sara joined Michael and his family in Colorado at Christmastime. Younger sister Elaine was reserved but polite, but Michael's mom was almost openly antagonistic. Returning to Chicago after three stressful days, Michael began to explain to Sara the nature of his relationship with the woman who so reminded Sara of her own mother. "She is just never happy— not with me, not with Elaine, especially not with herself. It is not surprising that she doesn't like you, Sara, because she doesn't like anyone." Then, he added, "That's why I haven't given you your present yet. I didn't want her to find something negative to say."

With that, Michael fumbled in his pocket for a small box wrapped as an obvious Yuletide gift. It was the first "Christmas" present Jewish Sara had ever received, and her hands trembled as she removed the wrapping paper. Inside was a key. "It's the key to my apartment," said Michael hesitantly. "I want you to live with me."

Sara was stunned. Never once during their five months together had Michael betrayed any thought of a more permanent future together, and Sara had carefully avoided the idea too. So, she surprised both Michael and herself when she said only one word: "Yes."

Only after she and Michael began to share a home did Sara discover that Michael had more than dreams about success. He was committed to the fulfillment of his dream through a regimen of long hours and dedication unmatched by anything Sara had ever seen. She kept her own job, awakening at six each morning in order to arrive for the opening of her office at eight. But when she arose, Michael had already been at work for an hour, and Sara would not see him until well after seven in the evening. Thoughts of the long hours of loneliness she had endured waiting for Stuart rushed back with a vengeance.

Although Michael kept to his schedule of a fourteen-hour day, never eating breakfast and often skipping lunch, Sara discovered to her relief that when he returned home, he was sober—and his attention was focused on her. Although he went to bed early each evening, for the two or three hours they shared together, they were a couple, relaxed and contented in the presence of each other.

During the spring and their first full summer together, Sara developed a routine that was comfortable, shared moments of joy with Michael, and continued to enjoy success at work. They had agreed to keep their finances separate, but Sara insisted on contributing to the household expenses. Still, she was able to continue building her own small investment portfolio, and she delighted each month in reviewing her statement. It was not a large amount of money, she knew, but it was hers, she was happy, she lived with a loving partner, and she was still independent.

Neither had thought through the decision they would face in the fall. The Florida-LSU game was the seventh of the season for both schools, both teams entered the fray undefeated, and their dual promise from the previous year hung in the air like a cloud before a rainstorm. On the Friday before the big game,

Sara finally broached the subject with feigned indifference. "What are we going to do tomorrow?" she asked. "We promised not to watch together, but this year, I don't have my own apartment."

Michael was stumped. He would not miss his favorite team, and his one extravagance had been a TV dish that would beam SEC games to distant Chicago. Their problem was solved by a short blurb during the sports news that evening. A small contingent of LSU *alumnae* living in Chicago had begun gathering together in a local tavern a few years earlier to watch their beloved Tigers. "That's it," proclaimed Sara. "I'll watch with them."

Entering "Tiger Town Midwest" the following afternoon, Sara was startled to discover almost two hundred Tiger supporters already well into a pre-game celebration. When the Tigers scored on their first possession, Sara joined the raucous celebration, hugging people she had never met and cheering wildly. But it was not the year of the Tiger. The Florida defense reverted to its familiar stingy habits, and LSU failed to score the remainder of the game. Three Gator field goals brought victory, and Sara drove home disappointed, hoping Michael would not be too overjoyed. They both learned something when she walked in the door. Sara realized she was happy for Michael even though her own team had lost. And Michael reciprocated. "Honey, last year, I realized that if we had to lose to anybody, I was glad it was your team. And man, I could not believe we never did score a touchdown score against that Tiger defense."

They had broken their agreement not to talk about the game, but they had grown closer to each other. No one lost that day. Throughout the years that followed, they watched football together, even games between Florida and LSU.

Both careers flourished. Sara kept moving up in her company and watched her personal nest egg grow. But she fumed silently each month when Michael sent almost half of his own income in alimony to his former wife. Then, he received two pieces of stunning news on the same day late in the fall. Sara, as was her habit, gathered the daily mail and separated out the items addressed to Michael, which she would hand to him shortly after he returned from work. When Michael entered, he accepted her proffer of his daily stack of mail and quietly handed her the letter he had received in his office late in the afternoon. As she read, Michael seemed to stare straight through her.

"Dear Michael," she read, "In recognition of your excellence at the position you currently occupy, the board of the corporation has promoted you to the position of senior manager of the western region with headquarters in Los Angeles." Sara read the details about the substantial salary increase, the bonus structure, and the management perquisites that accompanied the promotion. Responding to the wry smile on his face, Sara realized that Michael was waiting to share his moment triumph with her, and she threw her arms around his neck. "Honey, I am so proud of you," she whispered as she embraced him tightly. "No one deserves it more."

While Sara bustled about finishing supper, Michael began to sort through the mail Sara had handed him earlier. Although she knew that one letter carried the return address of his former wife, Sara had not mentioned it to Michael. When Michael read it, he marched quickly into the tiny dining room and interrupted Sara's attempt to set the table. "Well," said Michael as he looked directly into her eyes, "it gets better." With that, he handed her the letter that he had just read for the first time. As Sara read it, both she and Michael began to smile, then to laugh, then to dance around the living room together. "She's getting married!" Michael was literally shouting. "No more alimony." The two events together would more than triple his income.

Rushing into the kitchen, Michael began to transfer into plastic containers the food Sara had prepared for their supper. Sara watched with astonishment as he placed everything in the refrigerator. "Are you too excited to eat?"

"Hell no," shouted Michael. "But tonight, I'm taking my lady to the finest restaurant in Chicago." It was the kind of extravagance Michael rarely allowed himself, and Sara realized how heavy a financial burden he had been carrying. Their food that evening tasted better than any meal she had eaten in a long time.

As they lay quietly in bed later, Michael spoke. "You know I want you to come with me, don't you? I could not bear to be apart from you."

"I hoped you would feel that way," Sara responded. "But what about my job?"

"I can support us now," Michael assured her as he drifted off to sleep.

But sleep would not come for Sara. Her own career was important to her. It marked her independence, helped to define her self-worth, and was a living reminder of her own sacrifices in returning to finish her education and prove herself daily. Did Michael not understand? Did he think her work so much less important than his?

The following evening, Sara articulated her questions to Michael and was both gratified and terrified by his response. Of course he thought her career important, but thought he could not possibly forego the chance to move up so dramatically on his own corporate ladder. "Besides," he said stoutly, "we will be together, and that is the only thing that truly matters."

Something about his answer left Sara unsatisfied, something she did not identify until again the sleep fairy danced just out of reach as they lay in bed together. Something was missing, Sara knew. And suddenly, she found the answer. She and Michael needed to talk again, and though she feared the result of what she now recognized as the truth about their relationship, she saw no alternative.

The following evening, Sara again led the conversation. "I have considered your offer to accompany you to Los Angeles," she began. "And I am prepared to give you a conditional answer." Trying to ignore the anguished look on Michael's face, she continued. "I will resign my position and will go to Los Angeles with you as your wife but not as anything less."

Michael's shoulders sagged, and during the long silence that ensued he seemed unable to speak. "I thought you were happy," he said finally. "I thought we loved each other."

"I do love you, Michael," Sara responded firmly, "with all my heart. And now I am willing to link my future with yours completely, willing to abandon my own career, willing to do everything I can to support your dreams. But I need to know if the depth of your commitment to me matches that of mine to you."

Silence once again descended on the room. Finally, Michael spoke. "I swore I would never marry again, Sara. And I have always been honest with you about that. And you always have said you were afraid of marriage too." Sara's heart stopped as she waited for him to continue. It started to beat again with his explanation: "I know that marriage with you is less risky than life without you."

With that, Michael slid to his knees and looked straight into Sara's face. "Sara, will you be my bride?"

Sara's verbal "Yes" was matched only by the radiance of her smile.

Late that evening, just before Michael fell asleep, Sara heard herself phrasing another question in a way that surprised them both. "Shall I start finding a rabbi tomorrow?" she asked drowsily.

"A rabbi?"

"Of course. Every nice Jewish girl needs a rabbi for her wedding."

"Well, I hadn't thought that far ahead, but a rabbi will be fine, if we can find one who does inter-faith marriages."

Since Sara was not a member of any synagogue congregation, she knew that finding such a person would indeed be difficult, but she persisted and soon found herself seated across the desk from a sober-looking, grey-haired man who introduced himself as "Rabbi Silverman." As Sara explained her situation to him, the rabbi seemed impassive but attentive.

"It is possible that I can marry you, Sara," he responded quietly. "But before I do, I will need to speak privately with Michael, and he will need to convince me that he respects our faith and our traditions. Is he willing to that?"

The answer came two days later when Michael walked hesitantly into the rabbi's office. "Rabbi Silverman, I am Michael, Sara's fiancé."

Michael never told Sara the substance of his conversation with the rabbi, and she never asked. All Rabbi Silverman told her was, "I believe Michael is a fine and moral man, and I am certain that he is devoted to you. I am also confident that he will support your efforts to live as a Jew should you decide to do so. I will agree to marry the two of you. All that remains is for us to set a date."

One week later, Michael and Sara were married in a simple ceremony held in the rabbi's office. The two witnesses were Sara's mom, who was Michael's second-biggest fan, and a Jewish colleague of Michael from the office.

As they walked out of the rabbi's office hand in hand, Michael turned to Sara. "The wedding ring I just gave you is all I can afford now. But someday, I'll buy you a real diamond."

"I already have the only diamond I need, Michael— you." With that simple exchange, they went to dinner together for the first time as husband and wife.

Following their move to Los Angeles, the new couple lived comfortably but modestly on Michael's monthly salary, and when he received an annual bonus each year, he insisted that the entire sum be invested. For a time, because his first wife had been an irresponsible spendthrift, Michael watched the family budget carefully. But he soon learned that Sara, having grown up in a modest financial environment herself, was fully willing to share his conservative outlook. Even when Michael became confident that he could relax his vigilance about the amount of money Sara spent, she never took advantage of his generosity, never spent more than they had agreed. In addition, she dressed modestly, eschewing overpriced baubles and designer labels.

The new wife quickly learned that Michael lived strictly by several basic rules of finance, repeating his favorite maxims often. As they shared information with each other, he insisted that they pool everything together. And Sara, at first reluctant to lose control of her personal money, was startled to learn that

Michael had actually saved more than she had, even while paying alimony and living on only one-half of his income. When she wondered aloud how he had managed to save in such a situation, Michael revealed to Sara his secret. "It's not how much you make that counts," he asserted, "but how much you spend." He spoke of "the time value of money" and was fond of reminding Sara that "You never eat your chickens, only the eggs."

The result of their careful financial planning was dramatic. While other couples in the same income bracket spent every penny they earned year after year, Michael and Sara saved systematically and invested wisely. By spending Michael's entire income, they could easily have afforded a larger house, fancier cars, or ostentatious jewelry. But they never allowed themselves to fall into the trap of "keeping up with the Joneses," choosing to take delight in watching their nest egg grow steadily, often laughing at the "things" other couples bought each year, only to throw them away as soon as a new toy came on the market.

The Corporate Wife

Over the ensuing years, Michael's comfortable income and frequent corporate moves made it both unnecessary and impossible for Sara to consider working outside their home. She began instead began to develop other interests. When Michael became the CEO of a Fortune Five-Hundred subsidiary, Sara settled naturally into her role as his wife and confidant. The wives of younger junior executives looked to her for advice, and soon, she was busier than ever with social events, business trips, and big sister counseling. Whenever the wife of a new junior executive needed a friend, Sara was the inevitable choice. As she had cared about children and animals in childhood, so now she learned to watch for the signals that a young and frightened wife needed her support.

When a wide-eyed new wife confided in her that she was lonely because her husband worked such long hours that he returned home "too exhausted to spend time with me," Sara shared a special secret with her. "While John is away at work, invest your time in developing your own interests. Finish your college degree, volunteer at a health clinic, write a great American novel, do something you enjoy and that you know is useful. But don't just sit there and wait for your husband to make you happy." Then, she added what she herself had learned living with Michael. "When your husband gets home after a difficult day at the office, the last thing he wants is a wife who saps even more of his energy. If he finds a cheerful companion who is happy with her own success in life, you will become interesting to him, and he will want to spend time with you."

Sara was sharing with the younger woman the lesson she had learned the hard way. Michael had remained the poster boy for "Workaholics Anonymous," and the demands of his career sometimes left him wanting nothing more than to be left alone when he finished a day's work. Sara battled loneliness and the feeling that she and her husband lived in two separate worlds. Realizing that while Michael was growing and changing, she was simply letting time pass during his stressful work week, she decided to take matters into her own hands. She enrolled in a computer class at a small college nearby and soon became a whiz at using what was at the time a largely unknown piece of equipment. Returning from work one evening, Michael found Sara hard at work with a machine he neither cared about nor appreciated.

"What are you doing now?"

"Well," responded Sara, "I'm putting all our records on this new software. Look! It tracks everything we have spent for the past year, projects our income needs for the next twelve months, and analyzes all our investments. Here is our entire financial portfolio." Michael's eyes widened as he surveyed the screen on which every detail of their financial picture seemed magically to appear.

Sara was on a roll. "See, this stock has been doing poorly; these are doing quite well. Maybe we should think about making some changes."

Her enthusiasm was infectious, Michael was duly impressed, and the two spent the next hour poring over financial data complete with charts, graphs, and projections. Every question Michael had the computer could answer based on the information Sara had already fed into it. Her delight at doing something that interested and helped them both was palpable. When she confessed that she had forgotten to prepare dinner because of her computer fetish, Michael surprised her by responding, "No problem. I know a cozy little restaurant where we can get a great meal while we talk some more about our future." Sara had discovered an important key to her own happiness, and she had contributed to Michael's wellbeing at the same time. It was a lesson she never forgot.

At about the same time, Sara returned to an old love, horticulture and flower arranging. It was a hobby that her father had shared with her, and the opportunity to develop it as an adult proved to be an unending source of satisfaction and delight. But her hobby grew past all her expectations one evening at a party she and Michael hosted for company executives. "Sara, I have to have that arrangement for my mother's birthday party tomorrow," exclaimed the wife of a young manager. "My mother loves flowers, and I have never seen anything quite as beautiful as the way you have arranged these tiger lilies together."

Sara, as anyone who knew her would have known, graciously offered the arrangement as a gift to the younger woman, and she thought no more about it. To her surprise, when the phone rang on the following morning, the caller was the mother whose birthday had been the occasion of Sara's flower arrangement.

"Sara," the older woman gushed, "not only did your arrangement make my birthday special. My daughter tells me you do other kinds of decorations, like theme-setting entryways and centerpieces for large galas, mood lighting, party favors, waterfalls and fountains, and even costumes for servers to match. Several of my friends now want to hire you for their parties."

Sara was stunned. For years, she had been the first one called whenever Michael's company had a social event, and she was recognized as the company party decorator without portfolio. She was accustomed to hearing her efforts praised and often commented about the enjoyment she derived from accepting a challenging assignment. Since every occasion posed a unique set of problems—a limited budget, a short amount of time to prepare, a cramped space in which to work, no volunteer labor to assist—Sara had always thought the reward for her efforts was the thrill of seeing a finished product that she had designed and created bring pleasure to others. But she had never before charged for her services, and she had no idea how to set a fee structure. Still, intrigued by the prospect of doing something that required her special skills, she agreed to accept calls of inquiry from prospective clients.

Her first assignment involved the *bat mitzvah* of a young girl from a prominent family. During the ceremony proper, the young girl was scheduled to read the Genesis story of the meeting between Jacob and Rachel at public water well, the traditional scene of social intercourse in biblical stories. Assured by the wealthy parents that cost was not an issue, Sara directed workers to construct a stunning entryway into the social hall rented for the party held following the ceremony. Guests entered under an arch that was a replica of the archway often seen at Middle Eastern water wells. Placed atop the wall of the well itself, each group of guests found a small wooden water bucket with the name tags of their family, directions to their seats, and an elegantly printed menu and entertainment program. Lighting and flower arrangements for each table completed Sara's creations.

The evening was a complete success, and Sara's decorations drew rave reviews. She also handed out more than two dozen newly printed business cards to parents of future *b'nei mitzvah*, engaged couples, married couples with anniversaries approaching, and potential birthday celebrants. As the evening drew to a close, Sara presented to the father of the *bat mitzvah* a detailed listing of her expenditures for the party that failed to include an amount for her planning efforts. When the father handed her a personal check, the amount not only covered all her expenditures, but it also included a generous stipend for her.

"Truthfully," she explained to Michael in private, "I would have been happy with far less because I had so much fun doing the project."

"Don't ever let anyone else hear you say that," responded Michael with a wry grin. "The entire family is happy. And besides, I need a new sand wedge."

"Not on your life," retorted the new entrepreneur. "This money is all mine." She promptly stuffed the check into her small pocketbook and smiled sweetly.

That first assignment proved to be only a beginning. In fact, so frequently was she called upon to plan a new theme or to decorate for an exciting occasion that soon, Sara was forced to turn down more offers for jobs than she accepted. With her burgeoning profits, Sara converted the spare bedroom into a private space for her work and began to stock her new studio. She compiled a telephone contact list for every conceivable company that provided catering, lighting, decorating materials from small to giant-sized, and other necessities for her creations. Soon, she had stocked virtually everything she needed at her fingertips.

"When inspiration strikes," she explained, "I don't want to stop and run to a store looking for the right materials." It was the best of both worlds. She was doing something she truly enjoyed, and she was making money in the process.

In addition to stocking her first-class studio, Sara also increased the size of her *pushke*, the Yiddish word describing a special hiding place where married Jewish women traditionally secreted small sums of cash saved from the money their husbands gave them to run the household. The practice had begun hundreds of years earlier among poor Jewish families living throughout Europe, where the *pushke* was often the family's only emergency fund for doctor bills or other unplanned expenses. In time, it became customary for Jewish wives to stash their emergency money in knotted handkerchiefs that were easy to hide, and Sara also knew the Yiddish word *knipl*, a "knot," sometimes used as a synonym for *pushke*. But in her family, the word was *pushke*, and Sara's grandmother and mother had helped her create her own hiding place for extra cash even as a young girl.

Because Michael had always been generous with her, and because they had insurance and savings for emergencies, Sara had never needed to accumulate more than a few dollars in her *pushke*; the success of her new hobby produced enough discretionary cash that her *pushke* began to grow exponentially. As anyone who knew her would have understood, Sara seldom used her secret money to buy things for herself. Instead, she delighted in having the means to purchase special gifts for friends and loved ones. She even bought that new sand wedge for Michael!

"Motherhood"

Still, there was a cloud hovering over the relationship. Sara was growing older and desperately wanted to bear a child of her own. But Michael had two older children by his previous marriage, and he could not understand her deep-seated longing. And children were not in the grand design of God for Sara. Even when Michael consented to have her stop taking birth control pills, the longed-for pregnancy did not ensue.

So, eagerly seeking opportunities for surrogate motherhood, Sara turned to Michael's two children, whose own biological mother had exhibited little of what most people call the "maternal instinct." But her attempts met with little success, and Sara could not avoid the reason why. While Michael could be warm and fuzzy with an animal, tender and caring with her, he failed to grasp the secret of effective parenting. Instead of giving his son and daughter time and attention, Michael simply gave them material things, often spending surprising sums of money without consulting Sara. To her sorrow, she was forced to face the fact that Michael was using money to avoid the real needs of his children. His actions would come back to haunt them both.

　"Dad, I need money" became the repeated request from eighteen-year-old Michael Jr. and his sixteen-year old sister. To Sara, it sounded more like a demand than a request. Time after time, even after both children had married and started families of their own, Michael complied with virtually every demand. The results were predictable—and disastrous. Demands that were presented as a "loan" were never repaid. Money sent by Dad for the necessities of life was squandered foolishly on frivolous things. Business ideas were abandoned at the first sign of hard work; numerous "get-rich-quick" schemes proved baseless. What was worse, the children looked at Sara as a competitor for their father's money. As a result, they spurned her affection and shut her out of their lives.

　After one particularly egregious example of his children's wasteful habits, Michael grimly noted that their pet name for him was "ATM." But the next time a request for a "loan" was made, Michael again wrote a check, just one more "loan" that was unappreciated and would remain unpaid.

　When both of Michael's children drifted aimlessly into drug and alcohol addiction, the rift between Sara and them was complete. Not only would she remain unable to bear her own biological child. All efforts to mother her stepchildren were rebuffed. Sometimes, she thought, the universe could be an unfair place. Women with no commitment to the long-term demands of maternity were often blessed with fertile bodies, producing infants for whom they seemed incapable of providing adequate nurture and love. And sometimes, a warm and caring woman with the heart of a true "mother," a woman like Sara, was denied an outlet for her great love.

But Sara was still the little girl drawn to rescue any creature, human or animal, that was in distress. To her delight, she discovered that Michael loved animals as much as she did. Soon, their home was a virtual zoo filled with adopted cats, stray dogs, and one or two homeless birds. She and Michael made it a special point to keep extra food on hand, and many a hungry animal learned to seek out their yard. Even a wounded raccoon found itself rescued, nursed back to health, and welcomed into the neighborhood. One rescue mission produced eleven kittens from two different litters, and Sara poured into each animal the concern for the underdog that she had exhibited as a young girl. She bottle-fed the tiny kittens and reluctantly agreed to allow them to be adopted only after she had carefully "vetted" each family to be certain that they would care for each one properly.

In fact, observing Michael with animals helped Sara understand more about the man to whom she was married. Watching him cradle tiny kittens in his arms or romp with an excited puppy outdoors told her that his heart was pure. And besides, animals really were easier than children. They never asked for money!

Again, it was the Jewish side of Sara that took a backseat. True to the assurances he had given to Rabbi Silverman, Michael tolerated no hint of anti-Jewish attitudes among his friends and colleagues, and he remained proud of Sara's Jewish heritage. But he was a non-practicing Christian working in a Christian-dominant society, Sara still did not attend synagogue services, all their new associates were Christian, and Judaism receded yet further into the background. She never lost her fierce pride in being Jewish but still felt forced by her circumstances to forego any possibility of living and worshiping as a Jew.

Retirement

In 1992, twelve years into the marriage, Michael decided to retire early, a decision made possible by their careful financial planning and conservative lifestyle. It was only natural that he would choose to retire in Florida, the state in which he had been born, and for whose university he had starred as a hurdler. The beautiful town of Pensacola beckoned, and Michael found a peaceful residential lot bordering the second hole of the best golf course in the area. Michael and Sara built their dream home together, and they settled in for a life free of stress.

During the construction of their new home, Sara met the twelve-year-old son of their contractor. Every day, the boy trotted eagerly at his father's side, and seeing the two males together reminded Sara of the relationship she had enjoyed with her own dad as a young girl. When she asked him if he played football, his response startled her. "No, Ma'am," he said softly. "I have a weak heart."

That afternoon, the boy's father explained to Sara that Billy had a bad heart valve, and she became certain that he needed her special attention. Soon, she became Billy's second-best friend.

Late in August, in honor of Billy's birthday that would denote him an official teenager, Sara planned a surprise party to which she invited several of Billy's school chums. To the delight of the boys at the party, Sara announced that she was going to serve them champagne, setting real champagne glasses filled with sparkling cider in front of Billy and each guest. The boys soon pretended to be inebriated and embarked on a series of hilarious gestures, looking as if they were falling-down drunk. Billy's party was declared to be the coolest birthday bash ever, and Sara knew she had given him a special afternoon.

When their new home was completed, Sara discovered that the country club serving the golf course was populated with men a lot like Michael, successful business executives who wanted nothing more than to trade the high-stress environment of corporate America for a leisurely routine of daily golf followed by a few drinks in the clubhouse with the boys. Michael jumped at the chance for regular physical exercise and rapidly became one of the better golfers in the club, a status achieved through numerous lessons, long hours of practice, and a daily regimen of eighteen holes, routinely followed by cocktails and conversation with his new friends.

Sara had embraced Michael's idea of early retirement, assuming it would provide opportunities for the two of them to spend time together, but Michael's preoccupation with golf and socializing with the boys shattered that assumption. So, Sara tried golfing with the girls, other "golf widows," as they referred to themselves, and even tried her hand at tennis. Her natural athleticism allowed her to master both sports quickly, but her satisfaction was tempered by the discovery that her female sporting partners came in two forms—those who played poorly yet flew into a rage when they lost and those who had no intention of taking "just a game" seriously. When a tennis elbow plagued Sara, she abandoned both sports with scarcely a backward glance.

Her passion for reading returned, and she devoured literally scores of books—history, biography, fiction, and even a book or two about her beloved, dormant Judaism. She seldom left her home except to accompany Michael to a club party where the husbands drank and told war stories in one corner while the wives huddled together across the room, also drinking but mostly gossiping about someone's sartorial *faux pas* or a rumored affair. The spiritual dimension of Sara's life remained undeveloped.

Then, what began as totally frightening experiences, the frequent hurricanes that plagued the coastline of Florida, provided an opportunity for Sara to become heavily involved in the business of animal rescue. Families that were forced to flee during a storm often left animals behind to survive on their own, and Sara joined other volunteers in rescuing family pets whose families had abandoned them. On one of her frequent stops at the office of the veterinarian who assisted Sara and others in caring for and placing the animals, Sara's attention was drawn to a beautiful grey cat. "She just wouldn't stop looking at me," she explained helplessly to Michael. "I had to bring her home." Michael understood, and "Grey Girl" soon became the true ruler of the home.

It was the grey beauty who taught Sara something she had never realized before. On normal days, Grey Girl was Michael's cat, sitting in his lap as he read the newspaper in the morning, curling up with him for an afternoon nap, never leaving his side. But when Sara contracted a severe case of influenza, Grey Girl became her nurse. Confined to her bed with a fever, breathing only with difficulty, Sara had a constant companion. Grey Girl stayed with her for almost two weeks, comforting her, loving her, helping her recover. Only then did she return to Michael's side. "She knew," Sara told Michael. "I don't know how, but she just knew how bad I felt."

A terrible storm the following season left more animals in need of rescue. From two separate litters, a total of eight rescued kittens arrived in the home of Michael and Sara to be lovingly nurtured by Sara. Six were quickly adopted by acceptable families, but Sara could not bear to part with the remaining pair. Her special concern for one of the kittens had begun when a sudden noise sent seven of the babies scurrying for safety, and Sara noticed that only the solid white female seemed unconcerned. A simple test, clapping her hands sharply behind the kitten, taught Sara that "Ivory" was profoundly deaf. Michael was not surprised when Sara asserted that "Ivory needs me" and refused to consider any family hoping to adopt her.

But Ivory had a sister, "Ebony," as solidly black as Ivory was white. Ivory was adoring and sweet. Ebony was one hundred percent rapscallion. Sara simply had to keep Ebony, too, she explained, "because Ivory needs someone to play with." Michael merely smiled.

"Cougar," a border collie with enough energy to keep up with Ebony, became the champion and protector of all three cats. But first and foremost, Cougar loved Sara as Grey Girl was devoted to Michael. When she bustled about in the kitchen, Cougar matched her step for step. When she worked in her studio, he lay contentedly at her feet. They took long walks together and established the routine of watching for Michael to appear every morning on the fairway of hole number two behind the house, whereupon Cougar would bound out to greet him, returning only when Michael had finished putting and moved on to the next tee box.

With her books, her rescue activities, and her loving animals, Sara filled the hours while Michael played golf. Her life was full and rich, but she and Michael were together almost as seldom as they had been during his active career.

Her beloved father had died years earlier, and finally, Mom came to live with Michael and Sara. When Michael left early each morning to play golf, Sara and Mom spent the day together, and at least Sara was not alone. But the regular and groundless complaints of the parent grew steadily, sapping Sara's energy, trying her patience, and creating a barrier between mother and daughter. Mom had fallen into a well-known trap, reverting to her now-distant past, which caused her to view Sara as still a child. Needing her daughter's help but resenting her own lack of independence, the older woman criticized everything Sara tried to do.

Both women were brought harshly back to reality at the medical report that came following a routine physical for Michael. Cancer and its bitter sidekick chemotherapy crowded into the home. It took the efforts of both women to care for the patient—driving him to doctor visits, dispensing his medicine, sitting with him all night while he battled bouts of nausea. But Michael was far too tough to allow cancer to take his life without a fight, and he intended to win the fight. Gradually, the medical reports changed for the better until finally, the magic word—remission—could be spoken. Michael had won. Life could continue.

But things were not the same, as Mom's long, slow slide into the hellish depths of Alzheimer's taxed all three of them. Michael still left early each morning to play golf, and Sara struggled with her mother alone, enduring her bouts of rage, finding only small comfort in the few moments of lucidity that occasionally returned without notice, always to fade away as quickly and unexpectedly as they had arrived. As weeks passed by, Michael grew stronger, Mom grew worse, and Sara's reservoir of energy sank to its lowest point in years. She learned to steal moments of reading while her mother slept and merely survived the older woman's waking moments. Her weight dropped, as her energy continued to do, lower with each passing day.

Then, Michael's cancer responded. It had been knocked down but not out, and it fought its way back into his body, more virulent than before. This time, there would be no victory for Michael, and both he and Sara sensed the reality of their situation. How, she did not know, but from somewhere, Sara summoned the strength to care for two patients at once. Her time with Mom grew increasingly contentious, and only the love that continued to radiate from Michael sustained her.

Despite the evil intruder lurking in the shadow of their lives and the inevitability of its ultimate victory, Michael and Sara grew ever closer through long talks, shared memories of happier times, and the sweetness of their twenty-five years together. But when both Michael and Mom were asleep, Sara found herself uneasy and conflicted. Weakened physically and emotionally by the heavy responsibilities she carried, she was also spiritually deprived and began to think of her Jewish childhood. Lying alone late one evening, a familiar thought came to her mind. She could not remember the exact words, but she recalled from childhood the blessing offered by the rabbi at the close of each service. She struggled to recall the complete blessing, but she could summon only the final line: "May the Lord grant you *Shalom*." She wondered if these were merely words or if they could somehow be the reflection of an integral spiritual dimension in life that she had neglected for so long.

Loss Times Two

When the end finally came for Michael, Sara offered him the ultimate demonstration of her devotion. She brought him home from the hospital, stayed by his side night and day for the last week of his life, and gave him the gift of death with dignity in his own bed.

The three weeks that followed were a blur to Sara. She tended to funeral arrangements, oversaw the organization of business and financial matters, and put on a brave front. She forced smiles for virtual strangers who offered condolences and remained the picture of grace under pressure. All too soon, the visitors left, and she was alone with Mom, a child in an old woman's body, incapable of controlling her bodily functions, unable even to bathe or dress herself. Only God knew how long Sara could have continued such a task, and he mercifully set the time limit at three weeks. But mom's death meant more funeral arrangements, new financial matters to untangle, another brave front.

And then, I had driven her home, finding her the following morning still asleep from exhaustion and grief.

Coping with Loneliness

After listening to the story of her life, I watched sadly as Miss Sara's world continued to change. The friends Michael and she had known at the club had been couples that now found no time for an attractive widow. Even worse, more than one married man leeringly suggested a physical liaison that Sara found disgusting. Night followed day followed night followed day. Time passed, but Sara found no solace.

Michael and Mom had died during the summer. As fall approached, still searching for answers, Sara decided to find a synagogue where she could worship for the High Holy Days. She entered a sanctuary for the first time in many years on Rosh ha-Shanah, the Jewish New Year, hoping that perhaps she, too, could begin anew. Hearing the music, reading the liturgy with others who shared her spiritual values, Sara's heart stirred. But although she and the other worshipers shared many things in common, she was still a stranger to them. After the service, no one seemed interested in meeting her, and only a few people even spoke to her. She drove home more alone than ever before and never returned.

Over the following months, Sara tried more than once to find her way. She visited a Buddhist Temple but found it foreign and uncomfortable. She attended several church functions for "singles," only to learn that she did not fit there either. She was single in a couples' world, trapped in the buckle of the "Bible Belt." She was Jewish in a Christian-dominated society.

Little brother Isaac, now a successful attorney in Boston, made a suggestion. "There is a website exclusively for Jewish single people. Try it. You should not be alone." In desperation, Sara took Isaac's advice. Her picture on site attracted numerous would-be suitors, prompting email exchanges, a few phone calls, and even a date or two. But each new candidate proved to be unworthy—too pushy, too needy, too arrogant, too demanding, or simply too far away.

One over-confident phone contact who lived several hours away called her from his car on a Friday morning. "I'm halfway to your house, but I need specific directions. I know if we spend this weekend together, we will be wonderful together." Sara was horrified. She had not even met the man in person, had given him no reason to believe she was seriously interested in him, and could not believe his rudeness.

"Turn around, my friend," she barked into her phone. "If you show up at my door, I'll call the police." Where were all the really nice men anyway!

Little brother Isaac had another suggestion. "We have a second cousin in Baton Rouge. Why don't you visit her? There are two synagogues in town, and 'Auntie Sophie' knows everybody. Maybe you could meet some Jewish friends through her."

With no better alternative, Sara called Sophie and planned a visit to Baton Rouge, only four hours from her home. Finally, in the company of someone whom she trusted, Sara poured out her heart to the relative she had met only once previously.

"You need to talk to someone, sweetheart, and I have just the right person in mind. He's a rabbi, a well-known scholar, a kind-hearted man. He guided my son through his *bar mitzvah* training. I'm sure he would counsel you."

Sara was intrigued. Maybe she needed the wisdom of a rabbi who could point the way back into spiritual growth for her. "Is he single?" Why had she even asked!

"Well, as a matter of fact, he is. But he is not your type. At any rate, I don't think you need a suitor; you need a counselor."

Why not, thought Sara. "Okay. I'll meet him."

3

The Meeting

Of course Sophie had Dr. Broulliette in mind. She knew that he had faced his own crisis of belief as a younger man and that he, too, had been involved in an interfaith marriage. She was also one of the few people who knew that Baraq had lost his first love to a tragic death in Israel. And in truth, she could not imagine Baraq in a romantic relationship. He was just not the type to care about such things. He had let his thick beard grow long, his manner of dress indicated that he worried little about his appearance, and to the casual eye, he appeared quite fierce. He was always clean but a bit unkempt, and no one had ever seen him wearing a tie except on special occasions in the synagogue; the warm climate of south Louisiana allowed him to teach his classes wearing slacks or shorts, sandals, and a short-sleeved shirt. And since Sophie was mortally afraid of dogs, the idea of a somber, disheveled professor with a huge Bullmastiff trudging at his side conjured up absolutely nothing romantic in her mind. In fact, so ominous did Lilit appear to her that whenever she had brought her son Josh to visit Dr. Broulliette for tutoring, she had never entered his home.

More to the point, Sophie felt that Sara needed wisdom and spiritual guidance, not just another suitor. When Sophie showed Sara an old newspaper picture of the good professor, her initial reaction was exactly what Sophie would have predicted. "Wow! He looks scary." But since Sara was seeking a wise counselor, she readily agreed with Sophie that physical attraction was not a requirement. Besides, Sophie knew that Baraq was tough only on the outside. Inside, his heart was tender, and it was well known among the Jews of Baton Rouge that Baraq could not say no to a call for help, never refused an invitation to tutor a *bar mitzvah* candidate, always participated eagerly in synagogue social projects. In fact, when Sophie had called Baraq shortly after the devastation wrought by Katrina had dumped thousands of homeless New Orleanians in Baton Rouge, Baraq had taken two families into his rambling old house and had fed them for four months out of his own pocket until FEMA finally coughed up the assistance to which they were entitled. In short, Baraq was a *mensch*, the old Yiddish word connoting a true and honorable human being. Sophie also felt certain that Dr. Broulliette could answer any question Sara might have about life, grief, or Judaism. So, she punched Baraq's number into her cell phone and reached him on the first try.

"Broulliette," the deep voice rumbled.

"Hiya, doc," came the response. At the sound of a familiar voice, Baraq's tone softened instantly.

"How have you been, Soph? And how is Josh, that rascal son of yours? Is he keeping up his Hebrew?"

"We're both great, doc. But that's not why I am calling." Quickly sketching Sara's situation for Baraq, Sophie asked if he might be willing to speak with her. "Anything for you, Soph," he responded quickly. "You know that."

"Yes, I did know. But thanks. This lady really needs your help." After a few minutes of chitchat, Sophie told Baraq that she was handing the phone to Sara.

When he knew that Sara had taken the phone from Sophie, Baraq began without giving her a chance to greet him first. "Hello, Sara. Sophie tells me you and I need to chat."

Something in the voice, the deep rumble, the measured confidence, told Sara she had called the right person. If anyone could face her demons with her, surely, it would be the speaker of that voice. She was pleased but not really surprised that Baraq agreed readily to meet with her and found herself seated alone in his tiny university office the following afternoon, waiting for his class to end. As she waited, Sara allowed her mind to drift. How strange it seemed at that moment for her to be in the office of a rabbi. How welcome it would be to hear those words that she had claimed as her own from childhood but could no longer remember fully. As a child, she had only imagined that the rabbi spoke them to her. Now, perhaps another rabbi would repeat them, and there would be no doubt that she was the intended audience. "May the Lord grant you *Shalom*." A little Shalom would be nice right now, thought Sara.

The Rabbi and the Widow

When Dr. Broulliette entered, Lilit at his side, Sara was startled out of her brief moment of reverie. The man with the dog did not look like any rabbi she had ever seen before. Wearing his trademark short-sleeved shirt, shorts, and sandals, he looked like the picture of a grizzled archaeologist she had seen in magazines but nothing like the rabbis she had met. She could not know that to Baraq—the tailored suit gracing her slender figure, matching purse and shoes, professionally coiffed hair crowning her smiling face—she looked like one of those highly-paid professional models he often noted on the cover of some women's magazine.

Not the kind of rag Dr. Broulliette had ever bought, of course, but the kind placed so as to be impossible to ignore whenever he went through a grocery store checkout line.

His eyes seemed to look into her soul, and his proffered hand was hard as granite. "Hello, Sara. I am Baraq," he began, and his voice seemed somehow gentler in person than it had over the telephone. "What is it you wish to discuss?"

Some might have found his brusque opening unsettling, but Sara did not. To the contrary, his calm and purposeful demeanor reassured her. Looking straight into his eyes, she thought she sensed an old soul, someone whom life had treated harshly but who had punched back and triumphed. Dr. Broulliette seemed at ease with himself, confident without being arrogant, the kind of guide whose very presence seemed to say, "Follow me. I know where we are going."

Sara did not, could not, know what Baraq was thinking. Had she guessed, it would have been impossible for her to understand. Gazing intently at the beautiful widow, the lonely rabbi found himself wondering about his own demons and about the possible role Sara might play in his fight against them. But he was an experienced counselor, and he steeled himself, pushing thoughts of his own demons into the background as he focused on what she began to tell him about herself. Baraq listened intently as she spoke, becoming the impassive counselor whose only comments were brief:

"I see."

"Of course."

"I think I understand."

"Please continue."

From time to time, Baraq fit a short question into a momentary pause by Sara:

"What happened next?"

"What do you think that means?"

"How did that make you feel?"

"What do you think you should do?"

For more than an hour, Sara shared with Baraq the outline of her life, her grief, her uncertainty about the future, her longing for a return to Judaism.

When she finished, Baraq closed his eyes and leaned back in his chair, remaining motionless for more than a minute. Then, he spoke. "I know you realize that I have no answers. In fact, I doubt that there are answers to the questions you have raised. But Judaism is not about answers. It is about active participation in the struggles of our lives, being a player rather than a spectator. The journey is all we have, and from what I've heard this afternoon, you have been an exemplary traveler as a child, a wife, a friend. Perhaps it is time now for you to let go of your past and embrace your future. And I would think you should be confident of your ability to fashion a life that has meaning and purpose, for that is what you have been doing all of these years."

He paused before adding, "You have suffered, as have millions of other Jews. But you have survived. And that is what we Jews do better than anyone else."

Both Sara and Baraq smiled at this last sentence, recalling the Jewish insider joke about all Jewish holidays. "They tried to kill us. We survived. Let's eat!" And although Baraq had told her nothing profound, nothing she had not thought countless times before, hearing the words from Baraq somehow made her feel confident that he could help her find *Shalom*.

"I think you have identified the crux of the problem," Sara responded. "But I noticed that you spoke of Jews, plural. And I am only one Jew, virtually the only one in my neck of the woods. The closest synagogue is nothing like the one I knew as a child, and I don't know any of the members there. How can I draw strength from my connection with our people when my link to them is so long ago in my distant past, and I have not met any of the Jews in Pensacola?"

After pausing again before responding, Baraq asked about the possibility that Sara might wish to move to a town with a larger Jewish population, opportunities for worship and social interaction, scores of Jewish friends from which to choose. Without knowing why, he pointed out that Baton Rouge was a good example of such a place, home to two major universities with their attendant cultural and educational opportunities as well as two active synagogue congregations with a total of almost five hundred Jewish families, virtually all of whom Aunt Sophie knew quite well.

Sara was open to the idea of moving from Pensacola, for she herself had considered the possibility on many a sleepless night. She had thought of Atlanta, where she and Michael had spent a delightful year, but realized that she had made no Jewish friends there either. She had rejected Chicago because of its harsh climate, as well as Los Angeles with its traffic jams, smog, and intolerable, beautiful people. Mom and Dad were deceased, and baby brother Isaac lived in distant Boston, so New Orleans seemed pointless. But she had not even considered Baton Rouge. Its climate matched that of Pensacola, and she had learned to accept the heat and mosquitoes there. Thoughts of the opportunity to chat often with Baraq flitted briefly across her consciousness but quickly passed off her radar.

Baraq and Sara spent several minutes discussing the general idea of a move to a more attractive Jewish climate, and he finally glanced at his watch, shocked to learn how much time had passed. Realizing that a move from Pensacola would require major preparation and thought, Baraq addressed Sara's need for more immediate help by suggesting a list of books that he thought she might find appropriate. She had a lot to consider. As she rose to leave, he wondered if he would ever see her again.

He need not have wondered. The two scarred veterans, each the survivor of numerous harsh blows in life, had formed an instant bond. Sara believed that she would be safe with Baraq, that she could share her deepest fears with him, and that he would understand. Baraq did not know why, but Sara's voice had a hypnotic effect on him, allowed him to relax, even encouraged him to reveal his gentle side to her, the side his stern exterior shielded from the view of almost everyone else.

She was a troubled Jew. He was a rabbi. Of course he would try to help.

Friendship

As their initial meeting ended, they agreed to meet again, sooner rather than later. Two weeks later, Baraq drove to Pensacola at Sara's invitation, where they spent two long days conversing, first as counselor-client but soon as two friends who felt comfortable in each other's presence. Baraq, the most "proper" person Sara had ever encountered, agreed only after prolonged urging to sleep in Sara's guest room, safely located on the other side of her spacious home from the master bedroom where Sara slept. "I promise you will be safe," she teased, and she thought she saw the hint of a smile cross his craggy face. Truth be told, they scarcely slept at all during those two days, talking late into both nights, already old friends.

Remember me? Carlita?

Because I was cleaning house when he arrived, I met Dr. Broulliette on that first trip, too, and was amazed at how relaxed Sara was with him in the house. In fact, as soon as he had returned to Baton Rouge, Sara was anxious to fill me in on the details of their meeting.

Lilit was another matter. Her size and fierce mien frightened me, and it took several visits before I understood that Lilit was not a threat. In fact, the faithful canine seemed to want it understood that whenever I was not present to assist Sara, Lilit herself would shoulder that responsibility. Ultimately, of course, Lilit gained my confidence and seemed to be watching me intently whenever I was working around the house. As she had accepted Jeff at LSU earlier, so now Lilit signaled her approval of me in Pensacola.

And Baraq met the cats. Ever the quintessential dog whisperer, Baraq had not admitted to Sara that he had never owned or even petted a cat. Nor had he told her that Lilit was the smaller of the two dogs who shared his life, that the other one was a giant English Mastiff male. But Lilit offered her own surprise. During the first afternoon in Pensacola, she signaled her need to go outside just as Baraq's cell phone rang with a call from his son. Knowing that Lilit would not allow anyone else to accompany her outside, he was offering to call back in a few moments when Sara volunteered to go with Lilit. In amazement, Baraq watched as Lilit casually trotted outdoors alongside Sara. It was the first time the faithful dog had ever gone anywhere with anyone but Baraq. Watching Lilit and Sara together, free to take the call from his son, Baraq found a comfortable chair and had just settled down when a cat bounded in his lap. It was Ivory, the beautiful white cat who, Sara had explained, "is leery of everyone." But apparently, Ivory felt as confident of Baraq as

Lilit did with Sara, and she curled her body inside the crook of his arm, fixed her eyes upon his, and purred. The dog man was smitten. Sara and I laughed about that many times together.

In fact, while Baraq watched Lilit's obvious approval of Sara, Sara was giggling to herself at the sight of her grizzled new friend being charmed by the first cat he had ever petted. The trust shown by the two animals indicated to the two humans that they had appraised each other correctly. After all, dogs and cats know more than humans. A dog, especially one like Lilit, just would not be comfortable with a bad person. And seeing Ivory sleeping peacefully in Baraq's arms told Sara everything she needed to know about the heart of her new friend and advisor.

During subsequent meetings in Baton Rouge, Baraq's giant male English Mastiff Shimshon adopted Sara; whenever Dr. Broulliette was in Pensacola, Grey Girl and Ebony wiggled their way into the small corner of Baraq's heart that Ivory had left available.

It was also during that first meeting in Pensacola that Baraq began to address his new friend using the Hebrew pronunciation of her name, Sará, instead of the familiar English Sára. No one had ever pronounced her name in Hebrew before, but Sara loved the way it sounded on Baraq's lips.

Returning to the Synagogue

Passover was approaching that spring, and during their fourth or fifth meeting, Baraq surprised Sara with an invitation to share the traditional *seder* meal with his congregation and him in Lake Charles. Another surprise awaited her there. Baraq's congregants, long accustomed to his arrival accompanied only by Lilit, were genuinely delighted to meet their rabbi's new friend. It was the first time any of them had seen Baraq with a woman, and since all Jews assume that rabbis should be married, many imagined a relationship far different from the simple friendship the two were building. Sara easily identified their assumption and was amused. After two non-Jewish husbands, she thought to herself, her family would never believe that she could become involved with a rabbi. But she and Baraq were not "involved," so the thought passed quickly.

The Passover celebration brought back to Sara some of the most pleasant memories of her childhood. She recognized and joined in the singing of the traditional songs, listened once again to the familiar story of her people's ancient struggle for freedom, and felt for the first time in years that she was in a place where she belonged. Driving away together after the meal, Sara shared with Baraq the warmth she had experienced, the healing that was now beginning, and again they talked late into the night before settling into separate rooms in the motel where Baraq stayed on his regular bimonthly visits to Lake Charles.

Lying alone in her bed, but no longer lonely, Sara counted her blessings. She had a warm and true new friend in Baraq, and he had shared with her a congregational family very similar to the one with which she had celebrated special Jewish holidays as a child. In a way, Sara felt that she was finally ready to leave her own Egyptian ordeal in search of a new land of promise and hope. Her sleep that night was peaceful, and she awoke refreshed.

Baraq barely slept, and then, only fitfully. He had noted the ease with which Sara had blended in with his beloved congregation, and he realized ruefully that it had been many years since he had shared a *seder* meal with a special female companion. He had been leading the annual *seder* for years and in various locations, always surrounded by other celebrating friends and congregants who looked to him for spiritual leadership. But when the ceremony ended, he had always gone home alone. No matter how he tried, he could not deny the joy that Sara's presence at the *seder* had brought to him. Nor could he stop himself from hoping that Sara would be there to share future holidays with him. Friends like her, he assured himself, are rare.

When Passover ended, Sara returned to Pensacola and plunged into the preliminary planning necessary for moving. To Baton Rouge? The thought would not go away. But first, there was a house that needed a few touch-ups before it would do well on the market. Two weeks of activity witnessed a parade of workmen entering the house to paint, repair tiny leaks, touch up spots of cracked stucco, tighten hinges, and replace screens. When Baraq arrived for their regular counseling session, he was surprised and pleased at the changes to the house as well as the idea that they represented. And he tried not to think about how alluring Sara looked in a pair of jeans and a man's work shirt. Their conversation that weekend centered on a new future for Sara, whose past struggles seemed to be growing ever more distant.

When Baraq insisted on helping with the work, his efforts with a paint brush were a total disaster, and Sara laughingly suggested that he would have to take his shower outside. So when she mentioned needing a small side table for an overstuffed chair in the living room, Baraq's offer to make one for her sounded like a continuation of the joke about his ineptitude. The table was not mentioned on Sara's next visit to Baton Rouge, but when Baraq returned to Pensacola four weeks later, he appeared at the front door carrying an exquisite wooden object that was exactly what Sara had described. Inspecting it closely, she found every joint perfect, every surface as smooth as glass. "Why didn't you tell me?"

"Well," said Baraq, with a boyish grin, "I am not anxious to have it known that there is a Jewish carpenter in the neighborhood!"

But the house did not sell. Throughout the summer months, Sara's meetings with Baraq continued to alternate between Pensacola and Baton Rouge, between her newly updated and spacious home and his older, long-neglected place. They never discussed the issue, but while Baraq occupied Sara's guest room in Pensacola, she stayed at a nearby motel whenever they met in Baton Rouge.

On her third trip, Baraq had offered to fix supper for her at his home, framing the invitation as an opportunity for her to meet Shimshon, the 185-pound giant, and Ya'el, the young female in training to replace Lilit at some future date. Entering Baraq's living room, Sara knew that no woman had touched the place in years, and for some reason, the thought made her happy. She found herself thinking about how the furniture should be rearranged, noting the need for paint and newer fixtures, imagining what the house would look like once she finished with it.

Baraq gave no indication that he knew what she was thinking but kept popping up from his chair in the living room to trot into the kitchen. On the first trip, he checked the oven timer and started two cups of water to boil, added one cup of rice to the water, and set a timer for fifteen minutes. On his second trip, she could hear him mixing and stirring but resisted the urge to enter his lair and see exactly what he was doing. On the third trip, after a bit more stirring and a few clinking sounds, he called Sara into his kitchen and seated her at the table on which he had set simple dishes and silverware in place. Taking one of the plates, he retrieved a beautiful roast from the oven, a large slice of which he placed on the plate Sara now realized was hers. From the stove, he spooned up steamed rice that he covered with the thick, brown gravy he had prepared, added fresh snow peas and a slice of the bread that he had baked, and set the plate in front of Sara. He repeated the serving procedure for his own plate and seated himself across from Sara at the small table. "*Be-te'avon*," he said, Hebrew for *bon appétit*. There had been no appetizer, there was no salad, and there would be no dessert.

The food itself may have been simple, but the taste was zesty, reminiscent of the meals Baraq had eaten since childhood. The Cajun seasoning challenged Sara's taste buds, and she ate far more than usual. The minute she had finished the last bite, Baraq was on his feet clearing the table, insisting that Sara stay seated to enjoy her coffee while he washed and put away the dishes, sealed and stored the leftover food in the refrigerator, and completely scoured the stove top. He shrugged off her amazement at his kitchen skills with a simple wave of the hand. "My grandfather taught me to cook. Grandmother was gone so much that he learned as a matter of self-preservation. Besides, all Cajun men cook."

Sara could not resist. "You are going to make some lucky woman a wonderful wife." It was the first time she had seen Baraq blush, and she knew instinctively that it was time to move the conversation in a different direction.

New Beginnings

The coming of fall also heralded the season known in Judaism as the "Ten Days of Awe," or simply "The High Holy Days." These special days begin with *Rosh ha-Shanah*, the Jewish new year, and end ten days later with *Yom Kippur*, the "Day of Atonement," the most solemn and sacred day of the Jewish year. Even non-observant Jews, who almost never attend synagogue services throughout the year, seldom miss the High Holy Days. On Rosh ha-Shanah, tradition holds, God decides which individuals will have their names inscribed in the "Book of Life" for the coming year and which ones will not. It is a metaphor for the reality that life hangs in the balance on many occasions. But even after some names are written on Rosh ha-Shanah, those who have not made the list may "sweeten the divine decree" during the ten days immediately following. Beginning with an honest inventory of one's deeds throughout the year that is ending, sincere Jews endeavor to correct whatever errors they have committed and in particular are urged to seek forgiveness from those whom they have wronged. Then, having made peace on the human level, prayers of repentance offered to God can be heard and divine forgiveness procured on Yom Kippur.

The Ten Days of Awe are about a fresh start above all else, addressing past mistakes and misdeeds in preparation for a clean slate with God and man. Shrugging off her disappointment at the cool reception she had received in Pensacola the year before, emboldened by the way the people in Lake Charles had responded to her at Passover, Sara agreed to spend the High Holy Days worshiping with Baraq and his congregation. There, in addition to the opportunity to share the profound liturgy that had developed over thousands of years, she would also hear seven earnest sermons from Baraq, who would articulate his deeply held personal beliefs about sin and repentance, prayer and devotion, a new heart, a fresh start.

As Baraq spoke, Sara experienced again that childlike feeling that the rabbi was speaking directly to her. Who more than she needed a fresh start? And a fresh start was exactly what she intended to make.

Yet even in the face of her resolution, Sara found the drama of Yom Kippur daunting. Beginning, as do all Jewish days, on the evening preceding the actual calendar date, Yom Kippur requires observing Jews to fast for twenty-five hours and includes the obligation to sit through an exhausting litany of prayers and sermons beginning in the evening and lasting throughout the following day. But Baraq reminded the congregation that fasting and prayers were not the only Jewish traditions, noting that the Tanna'im, the rabbis who had authored the Mishnah almost two thousand years earlier, had also banned drinking [even water], bathing, the use of perfume or other bodily ointments, leather footwear, and sexual intercourse.

"All in all," said Baraq as he concluded his remarks to open the evening service, "by the time the ancient rabbis were finished, not only would any Jew attempting to follow all of their restrictions feel appropriately sober, any congregant seated next to someone who had not bathed, brushed his teeth, or used deodorant would also experience the true meaning of the kind of affliction that leads to sincere repentance." It was a rare moment of levity to begin a solemn, daunting liturgy, and Sara had never heard a rabbi begin Yom Kippur in that manner.

As the afternoon service approached on the following day, Sara wondered how even Baraq could hold the attention of his tired and hungry congregants who had now missed both breakfast and lunch. She was to discover that he was up to the task. In fact, long after she heard it, she felt that she could remember almost every word of his powerful message based on the Book of Jonah. As she recalled it to me, these were his very words.

"Here we are in the middle of the most solemn day of the year, fighting fatigue and hunger, thinking about the most profound issues in life, and we take time out to read a silly story about a big fish swallowing a prophet. Surely, we are missing something.

Okay. Let's think about the story of Jonah in a slightly different version. Imagine that you are a family living in Assyria (we call it Iraq today). After a long week of work and worry, you decide to take a short break on the beach. You pack a nice lunch, include adequate liquid refreshments, plenty of towels, the biggest blanket you own, a bit of sunscreen, and a Frisbee. Then, you hie off with the children and the family dog in tow to relax. After too many sandwiches and too much sun, you lounge on the blanket and let your mind drift.

And then, it happens. The water begins to roil, until suddenly the surface is broken violently as the largest fish in the world shoots skyward from the water.

At the peak of its arc, the great fish vomits with a disgusting belching noise, and a large object hurtles forth from its mouth. You watch as the object sails upward before plunging into the sand close to your startled family. And then, you notice that the projectile is shaped like a human being, a man, who staggers to his feet, pulls seaweed from his face, wipes off the gunk that had attached to him in the belly of the fish, and turns in your direction. Fastening his eyes directly on you, the human projectile screams at the top of his voice: 'Repent!'"

As the congregation roared with laughter, Baraq noted solemnly, "I guarantee you that I would repent on the spot!"

Then, he continued. "Now surely, the ancient writer of this short story realized how utterly fantastic his yarn would sound. And I believe he used this literary setting to grab our attention and force us to focus on something far more important than a vomiting fish. So we read the story again, this time hoping to discover a clue to the true purpose of the author. And there it is, wrapped in the one word guaranteed to make us listen to the author's message. That word is Nineveh. Yes, Nineveh, the capital of the most savage people in world history, the hated terrorists who had toppled our beloved Israel and ravaged the countryside, looting, raping, and killing in the most violent fashion imaginable. The bellies of pregnant women were ripped open, killing both mother and child with one swipe of the sword. The heads of small children were dashed against rocks. Captured males were skinned alive and hanged on poles to die a slow and agonizing death. Nineveh was Assyria, the Al-Qaeda of its day, far more organized and efficient but equally deadly, heartless, and cruel.

Can we doubt that the author of Jonah succeeded in capturing the complete attention of his audience? What in the world could Jonah have to say about people like this? And then, we discover other words tucked away in the heart of the narrative.

'Repentance' leaps from the pages first. Now, we know that the Assyrians were not prone to make apologies. In fact, the description of their cruel methods comes from the records that they left in pictures and writing. They were not sorry for their deeds; they were proud of them! So where does 'Jonah' get off linking Assyria and repentance? We have to read further.

And thus, it is that a second key word comes to the fore—'forgiveness.' Now, forgiveness is a beautiful concept most of the time, but the very idea of the word used in the same sentence with Nineveh conjures up an absolutely awful thought. Surely, the God of justice would never forgive cruelty of such magnitude! Jonah must have been wrong, and in fact, other biblical prophets had taught that he was indeed off the mark. Take the prophet Nahum for example. He had devoted a long poem to the glorious concept of divine justice crushing mighty Assyria: humiliating her pagan gods, throwing her army into mass confusion, destroying her king in his own palace, plundering her treasure, dashing her children to violent death, and finally bringing her reign of terror to an ignominious end. Such a scene, said Nahum, would be an occasion of such great joy that everyone who heard the news would clap their hands in glee. Only such a conclusion could preserve the justice of God. Evil of Assyrian proportions simply had to be punished.

Obviously, Nahum was correct about Assyria, not Jonah.

So we look once again, more carefully now, at the story of Jonah. And finally, we discover one more key, this time a concept borrowed from the Book of Exodus. God, the God of justice, the God who demands that repentance be made for sin, is also 'gracious and compassionate, slow to anger, abundant in loving kindness, One who relents concerning calamity.'

By requiring us to consider the true character of God, Jonah has forced us to face the power of his message. Repentance works forgiveness. No evil is greater than the compassion of God. No sin stands outside his power to forgive.

And it is only when we grasp the power of divine compassion that we can appreciate the genius of Jonah. He took a concept that was impossible for the average person to conceive and fashioned it into an idea that gives meaning to all of our prayers on Yom Kippur. If God could forgive the worst people on earth, surely there is reason to believe that we, too, may find his forgiveness. Our prayers have not been in vain; our time has not been wasted. We are accomplishing something real and lasting.

As we approach the end of these exhausting 'Days of Awe,' we rejoice in the confidence that our own lives have been cleansed by the God who can forgive even Nineveh. We can start over with a completely clean slate, a clear conscience, with hearts purified by the awesome touch of the great and compassionate One whom we call 'our God.'

Now we know why we read Jonah every year."

Even though she had laughed along with the other congregants at the comical description of the belching, vomiting fish, Sara knew that the message of Jonah had reached her soul. Silently, she breathed a prayer and vowed to release the anger and the resentment she carried. As she prayed, she was certain that God had forgiven her, but more importantly, that she could forgive God. In particular, the idea of a "clean slate" seemed to her nothing less than a special gift from God. Recalling Baraq's words to her during their very first visit, she knew that her own heart was pure, her mind open to the possibility of new life. In Baton Rouge? With Baraq? Well, a girl needs a friend, she told herself quietly.

A Two-Way Street

But even as Sara was learning from Baraq, he was being transformed by her. She mentioned his thick beard only once and was stunned when he had trimmed it neatly at their next meeting. The shorter beard took years off his appearance, revealed more of his smile, framed the chiseled contours of his face more clearly. When she complimented his new look, he responded. "Thanks. I didn't want you to be ashamed to be seen with me in public."

In fact, Sara thought, he actually is quite a nice-looking man—for a friend! More surprises followed. Baraq bought several new shirts and seemed to take a little pride in his appearance. He no longer wore his black *kippah* everywhere, making him more approachable in her estimation. He became relaxed, smiled often, and seemed more at ease with each passing day.

But Sara knew only she was being allowed to see that underneath Baraq's scholarly exterior, there lurked a silly, boyish heart that saw humor everywhere. Observing him lead a public service, only Sara realized how hard he had prepared, and she alone knew that he battled nerves before approaching the podium—just like normal folks would. And perhaps only Sara could have convinced him to let people learn who he truly was.

In an unguarded moment, Baraq had confessed to Sara that his former wife had been uncomfortable with him, noting that she had thought his devotion to Judaism pointless and his brand of humor tasteless. Above all, he had noted, "She just really did not like me."

Her constant criticism had caused him to erect a protective barrier. With people around, Sara noticed, Baraq measured each word carefully, unwilling to risk allowing anyone to know what he was really thinking. When a joke was told, Baraq would smile politely but never laughed aloud, ever the overly-serious professor approaching life with earnest and determined steps. Yet Sara noted in their private meetings how frequently he phrased simple concepts in ways that were nothing short of hilarious. Solemnly attributing humorous statements to his grandfather, always keeping a straight face, he uttered many a memorable line.

And Sara found herself wishing that other people could see in Baraq the gentleness but especially the humor that he had become willing to reveal only to her. She thought of the addled waitress who had scrambled their orders, neglected to bring their silverware, and brought them drinks that another table had ordered. Most men, Sara thought, would have reacted with anger and criticism, probably demanding to see the manager. But Baraq had simply noted: "*Pour cette fille, il est toujours midi a quatorze heures*," which her college French helped her to translate: "For that girl, it is always noon at two o'clock."

He granted an interview request from the host of a local radio program with the wry comment that "I have a face made for radio," described an overly talkative colleague as "almost out of oxygen," and declared that his most peculiar neighbor was "waiting for spare parts from the planet of her origin."

And, Sara noted, Baraq was equally ready to laugh at himself. After spilling a full cup of coffee early one morning, he silently cleaned up his mess and refused to refill his cup with the comment, "I'm too stupid to drink coffee." Smashing his thumb with a hammer one afternoon, he had once again invoked his beloved grandfather. "Mr. B always said, 'If you're going to be stupid, you've got to be tough.'" At the time, Sara recalled, he had looked anything but tough. In fact, watching him suck his pulsating thumb while hopping on one foot, he looked much more like a frightened little boy than a fearsome professor!

Best of all, Sara noticed that Baraq's newfound self-confidence made other people at ease with him. At dinner one evening with several congregants, Sara insisted that he share the funny story he had told her earlier. After his account, delivered with flair and verve, their dinner companions convulsed with laughter, and Sara felt a sense of accomplishment that they were beginning to enjoy the lighter side of their beloved rabbi. The tender girl who had comforted frightened children and adopted wounded animals watched as her wounded friend came out of his defensive shell with her encouragement.

In fact, under her gentle guidance, emboldened by her ready acceptance of his true personality, Dr. Broulliette became "Baraq." He, too, was making a fresh start, becoming again the carefree and lighthearted person he had been as a young child, the fun-loving person his children had known as Dad. "Dr. Broulliette," the serious rabbi, had attended many a function as the main speaker, to offer a benediction, or to bless the occasion with a special *berakhah*. Now, "Baraq" was eagerly sought as a guest because he was a joy to have around. And Sara could not avoid the thought that many of their private meetings involved pleasurable activities with no counseling purpose at all. In fact, Sara was answering the question that had occurred to Baraq on their first meeting. She was helping him fight the demons of his past. She was changing him. And she was beginning to experience feelings for Baraq that made her happy, almost giddy. She was too cautious to allow such feelings to surface, but they were undeniably present.

Hanukkah

Hanukkah was the next holiday shared by the two friends. And Sara received her first gift from David, a sterling silver star of David to wear around her neck. Touched that he had wanted to give her a present, even more that it had been such a personal gift, Sara allowed to the surface an idea that had been submerged in her unconscious thoughts for months. What if? What if Baraq were feeling the same things she was feeling? Could he become more than just a friend? Over the succeeding weeks, she tried, always unsuccessfully, to ignore the thought.

But if Baraq was struggling with similar ideas, Sara had no way of knowing. He was always polite, always, as his adopted daughter Abigail phrased it, "proper." And yet, he seemed so at ease with her that Sara had to wonder what he truly thought about when they were together—and when they were apart.

Purim

The festival of *Purim* brought a new experience both to Baraq and Sara and to the Lake Charles congregation. Traditionally, Purim celebrations are designed to remind Jews of the first governmentally sponsored effort to exterminate them as an entire people. It is also the one event each year which Jews celebrate with silly costumes, sillier plays, and a raucous atmosphere. It is customary for rabbis to show their lighter side at Purim, not unusual to see a staid spiritual leader wearing a Queen Esther costume or drinking too much wine during the process of retelling the story of the Jewish Queen who saved the Jews from an evil foe named Haman. Not in Lake Charles. During Baraq's first Purim there, he had set a different tone, reading the entire

Book of Esther from the Bible before offering a scholarly lecture
on the evils of religious and ethnic prejudice. But that rabbi had
been "Dr. Broulliette." Sara was determined that the people in
Lake Charles would enjoy Purim this time with the rabbi who
had become "Baraq."

At her urging, with vocabulary help from his adopted
daughter Abigail, Baraq rewrote the biblical book of Esther in
modern idiom that teenagers could appreciate. The synagogue
president, a well-known attorney, was drafted to depict the evil
Haman, a serious professor of physical science became
Mordecai, Abigail the beautiful Queen Esther, his niece. Also on
the bill were a buxom lady playing the deposed Queen Vashti,
who sang "I Enjoy Being a Girl" while dancing an outlandish
routine, a demure school teacher acting as Haman's wife, another
prominent lawyer who played the court jester, and several teens
who filled various roles as advisors to the king. Baraq agreed to
play the role of the Persian King Ahasuerus and allowed Sara to
design a costume consisting of a comical bathrobe and a
ridiculous feathered crown purchased at a local costume shop.
He even succumbed to Sara's insistence that he perform several
rock and roll songs on the piano. She knew that his raucous
renditions would shock the congregants, who had no idea that he
played.

In the biblical story, Mordecai is rewarded for having
saved the life of the king by being placed on the king's own royal
steed and paraded through the town. Since a horse in the
sanctuary was too much even for Sara's fertile imagination, Lilit
was drafted. Instead of a ride of honor on the king's mount,
Mordecai's reward from King Ahasuerus (Baraq) became the
opportunity to take the royal lap dog on her daily walk. Lilit,
attired in a purple tutu, paraded through the congregation

followed by president "Haman" with an imaginary pooper scooper. She stole the show.

And Sara was tapped to serve as narrator. But not just any narrator. Borrowing a suit from Baraq, which hung on her slender frame like an amorphous tent, Sara added a bald cap to cover her hair and placed a *kippah* rakishly on top. When she glued on a thick grey beard and moustache, she appeared to be a comical little man who might actually have been Baraq's odd brother. And that gave the two conspirators another idea. They entered the synagogue from the rear together, Sara in costume, Baraq attired in his customary conservative suit. Sara remained hidden when Baraq went to the platform to begin the service. No one except the other actors in the play knew what was planned.

Walking to the pulpit, Baraq began solemnly, though lying through his teeth, to explain to the congregation that he felt it improper for a rabbi to act silly in the sanctuary, producing numerous frowns of disapproval from members who sat before him dressed in the costumes of ancient characters as disparate as David the shepherd king and Jezebel the licentious queen. Keeping a straight face, Baraq announced that his brother, also a rabbi, was visiting and would join him in leading the service. Surprised congregants, who thought correctly that Baraq had no brother, buzzed.

But Baraq was not finished. Pretending to receive a call on his cell phone, he announced that he had been called away on important rabbinical matters and asked his "brother" to lead the service without his help. He then hustled to the back of the synagogue to change into his Ahasuerus costume, while Sara bounded onto the platform. Her appearance prompted gasps of surprise, and her opening line, "Hallo, Temple Sinai," delivered with a thick Yiddish accent, certified her as the kind of family member Baraq had been wise to keep under wraps. So convincing was her costume that most of the people in the audience still had no idea that the "brother" was actually Sara and did not realize that they had been duped until the play was well under way.

Sara began by introducing "The Yid Kids," purportedly a famous acting troupe from Israel, and the characters for the play dashed through the startled congregation and up onto the platform. Their performance was riotous throughout. When the storyline arrived at the point where King Ahasuerus seeks a new queen, Baraq was led through the congregation ostensibly in search of the perfect candidate.

Turning first to a beautiful artist who was taller than he was, Baraq turned a deaf ear to her pleas: "No," he replied sarcastically to the advisor who had brought him to her for consideration, "she's too short to be a queen!"

Advancing down the aisle, a mother who approached him in the company of her young daughter was brought for his inspection. "Hmm," mused Baraq, stroking his beard. "I know I am only a stupid Persian king, but I don't think she is a virgin!" The audience gasped—and then roared.

The next candidate was a recent convert to Judaism whom Baraq rejected because "She looks too Jewish."

Near the back, the matriarch of the congregation, an impeccably dressed and elegant lady who was ninety years of age, was summoned. Baraq's assessment? "I think she's too much woman even for a king." As the congregation quaked again with laughter, Miss Rebecca attempted to frown, but it was clear that she relished the attention.

Now, Baraq appeared stymied and seemed to search the sea of faces with no luck. Then, his own seventeen-year old daughter was led by the hand to him by the royal advisor who was leading the search party. One look at Abigail, and Baraq made his choice. "Behold the new queen," he roared. Abigail blushed, and the audience cheered.

The play was a huge success, and the transformation in Baraq, accomplished under the careful tutelage of Sara, seemed complete.

Friendship in Jeopardy

Following their joyous and triumphant Purim performance together, Sara was exhilarated. Returning to Pensacola, she rested, read, and anticipated her next conversation with Baraq. A thoughtful member who had filmed the play sent her a DVD which she watched every day. Seeing Baraq obviously enjoying himself gave her the feeling that he was there with her.

Sara did not know that Baraq, too, watched the DVD repeatedly. Nor could she have guessed that the more he watched, the more uneasy he felt. He was a professional, he reminded himself. And a professional, a rabbi, a counselor, does not miss a client in the way that he missed Sara. It was a feeling that he could not shake.

A funeral for a congregant kept Baraq from keeping their standing appointment in Pensacola, and Sara arrived in Baton Rouge not having seen her friend for a full month. It was the longest they had gone without seeing each other since they had met, and Sara had eagerly anticipated their reunion. To her dismay, Baraq seemed different—distant, preoccupied. As was their habit, they talked long hours together, but the atmosphere was not as free and easy as before.

Baraq made no offer to explain the difference, and Sara did not press. But she returned to Pensacola feeling uncertain of what was happening, unable to shake the feeling that their regular bimonthly sessions were in jeopardy. Had he not enjoyed their Purim experience together? Was he ashamed of having shown his raucous, silly side to his congregants? Was he disappointed in the silly way Sara had acted as his "brother?" She decided to address the issue when Baraq came for their next meeting.

Sara never dreamed that the joint Purim performance that had left her exhilarated had brought waves of painful and frightening memories flooding back to Baraq. He was forced to admit to himself that his feelings for Sara were deeper than anything he had known in years. And those feelings, so familiar from his past, filled him with a sense of uneasiness that bordered on sheer panic. Thoughts of Leora came rushing back, memories he had carefully avoided for years. And Lyn's face haunted him as well, accompanied by the regrets that had followed his abandonment by Abigail's mother. All the women he had loved had left him.

Leora had loved him, of that he was certain. But she had died tragically before that love had been allowed to blossom into a life together. Lyn had loved the man she had hoped he might become but had been unable to accept his inability to become what he could not be. Abigail's mother had simply used him to find a father for her own child, and Baraq knew that she had not loved him enough even to attempt a lasting relationship.

And now, there was Sara. Baraq knew that he had become an important component of her new life, knew that she relied on him, saw that she needed his companionship as he relished hers. But he was forced to admit to himself that he had allowed himself to think of her as more than a counselee, more than just a friend. He knew that he had stepped over the line from friendship to something far deeper and realized that he could never return to the parameters of their original relationship. And he was certain that he and Sara viewed the world through different lenses. Their differences were surely insurmountable. She came from the world of corporate culture; he was a simple scholar and rabbi. Their financial situations were different. Their personalities were polar opposites. No, Baraq knew, they simply did not belong together in the kind of relationship that he had come to imagine. He could not bear another heartbreak, nor did he want to see the look on her face when she learned the truth about his feelings for her. An honest counselor, a true friend, Baraq knew, would not embarrass a lady like Sara.

Baraq's call on Thursday, the eve of his regular trip to join Sara in Pensacola, was even more puzzling and troubling to her than his changed attitude had been at their last meeting. Sara was certain that he was not telling her the true reason for his cancellation of their session, and the fact that he was unwilling to be completely honest with her bothered her more than the fact that she would not see him at the usual time. Again, she wondered what she could have done to disappoint him and spent the weekend alone in quiet reflection.

When Baraq called the following Tuesday morning, her trepidation grew. "I have to see you tonight," he said quietly, "on a matter of signal importance." The voice was once again that of Dr. Broulliette. Baraq seemed to have disappeared.

4

The Miracle

S ara knew that Tuesdays and Thursdays were the days on which Baraq taught his classes and that he could not leave Baton Rouge until sometime after 5:00 that evening. Knowing that he would not arrive until late, she faced a long day of continued bewilderment. "Signal importance," he had said. What could that mean?

"Carlita," she confided to me, "I don't know what has happened. I think Baraq is angry with me, but I don't know why." As we sat together in her home, Sara reviewed with me the most recent events in their relationship. She paused when I started to smile.

"You realize that you are in love with this man, don't you?"

My question that was not really a question seemed to startle her. "I don't think that is possible," she responded. "We are just friends. And besides, Baraq doesn't view me like that. To him, I am someone who needs help to reorient her life, especially in finding the way back to my roots in Judaism. He is a rabbi. Helping people is his job."

As I continued to smile, Sara mused further. "You may be correct. Maybe I have done what so many clients do with counselors. I think it is called 'transference.' I need someone in my life, and I have allowed myself to believe that the professional who listens to me and seems to understand my problems is the person whom I love. How silly is that!"

I said no more, but I thought back to the times I had observed the two of them together. That Sara was in love with Baraq I did not doubt. And it became clear to me that perhaps he, too, had made the mistake Sara was admitting to herself of having made. Maybe they both had crossed the line. Maybe they were in love with each other. Sure, he is a rabbi, I reasoned. But he is also a man. And what man could not love Sara? To me, they seemed perfect for each other.

I figured it would be wise for me to keep such thoughts to myself as I watched Sara attempt to stay busy while the hours crept by. But I found myself hoping that neither of them would do anything foolish.

The Moment of Truth

That same evening, the man standing at her door, arriving to discuss the "matter of signal importance," was not the person Sara had come to know. His countenance appeared to have been carved out of granite and then set resolutely to face an unpleasant and difficult task. His body was stiff, his demeanor wholly serious. Dr. Broulliette was standing there, not Baraq.

Sara's greeting surprised her more than it did him. "Come in, *Dr. Broulliette*," she said softly. Her voice trembled, tinged with a sadness she had not felt in months.

Once inside, she handed him a cup of coffee and watched silently as he settled into his favorite chair. Clearly, he was no longer at ease in her presence. Twirling the cup slowly in his hands, he waited for an eternity to speak.

"Sará," he began hesitantly, "I think our sessions have accomplished their purpose. You have grown more this past year than any individual I have ever counseled. It is time for you to be on your own, to become the strong and independent person you need to be."

Sara felt that she could not breathe. But she spoke not a word. "I know it may seem abrupt," the rabbi continued, "but it is only fair for me to tell you why I have come to this conclusion." Pausing to take his first sip of coffee, Baraq looked like a man who was drowning. It was the first time Sara had seen him at a loss for words.

"I have committed the unpardonable sin of the counselor," whispered Baraq. "I have fallen hopelessly in love with my client." The words did not register immediately with Sara, and she only heard but did not comprehend his continuing explanation. "I cannot be objective, can no longer focus on your needs because ... because I am consumed with my own desperate hunger simply to be in your presence." Fumbling for a way to continue, he was unable to summon another word.

Another pause followed, stretched into another eternity.

Sara tried to breathe. Baraq's face remained impassive.

Sara broke the silence. "Have you eaten?"

"No, but I am not hungry," said Baraq, not sharing the full truth that it had been more than seventy-two hours since his last bite.

"Well," said Sara quietly, "I guess we should get some rest. You have a long drive and should probably leave early."

"Of course," said Baraq, and he turned to the guest bedroom where he always slept, not trusting himself even to watch as Sara disappeared down the hall.

...

The two friends both found sleep impossible. Baraq simply stared at the ceiling, seeing nothing, feeling nothing, unable to think.

Sara lay quietly for a few moments and then began to weep softly.

Both Sara and Baraq wondered how a beautiful friendship could have created such misery. Baraq cursed himself as he thought bitterly of how foolish he had been. Sara curled herself into the fetal position and could not staunch the flow of tears.

After a few moments, Baraq felt a slight movement near the top of his chest, and he turned his eyes to the almost malevolent stare of Ivory, who was lying prone on his torso with her eyes locked onto his face. The loving cat seemed to be chastising him, and the intensity of her gaze disturbed him. He could not remember when she had entered his room.

At that moment, Sara also became aware that she was not alone in her bed. Reaching one hand from the locked position around her knees that she had tucked under her chin, she felt the massive body of Lilit and instantly cradled the dog's head against her bosom. "I'm going to miss you, big girl," she whispered as Lilit bathed her entire face with a loving, wet tongue. Then, the dog began to keen, the mournful sound literally piercing Sara's soul.

"It's okay, girl," said Sara. "I'm going to be okay."

But she was not okay, and her heart grew heavier with each labored breath. Then, new words spilled out, words she was incapable of controlling. "I love him too," she confided to the beautiful animal. "I love him too."

Hearing her own words, Sara began to smile. Then, she laughed, her entire body convulsing as a crescendo of mirth burst from her throat, producing a series of staccato barks from Lilit. Lying on the other side of the house, Baraq could not keep from hearing the mournful duet coming from Sara's bedroom as it morphed into a symphony of joy, and he realized for the first time that Lilit was not in the room with him. Hearing the only reaction he had not expected from Sara, he scrambled to his feet in total confusion. But he took not a single step.

Able to control herself only after an extended period of raucous laughter, Sara continued explaining herself to Lilit. "Hey, I broke the rules," she announced. "But so did Baraq. And since both of us crossed the line, the line will just have to be changed."

Bounding out of bed, Sara marched resolutely down the hall with Lilit hard on her heels. She burst into Baraq's room to find him standing, still in shock at the sounds of laughter that now followed Sara and Lilit until they both stood directly in front of him.

"Tell me something, rabbi." Her voice crackled with energy, and Baraq had never heard Sara use the tone of voice with which she now addressed him. "If you have committed the unpardonable sin, and I have committed the same sin, doesn't that mean we belong together?"

When Baraq started to respond, but only opened his mouth without uttering a single syllable, Sara answered her own question. "Silly, silly boy. My precious Baraq. Don't you know that I have loved you from the first minute we met!"

With those words, an admission made freely for the first time both to herself and to Baraq, she rushed to embrace him, her supple body pressing against his with a fierceness he had never experienced from any woman in his life, her lovely face buried in his neck. But even as he returned her embrace, Baraq was incapable of comprehending the meaning of the moment.

Baraq wondered if she would ever release him and finally grasped both of her wrists gently to enable himself to take a small backward step. As his opening words of the evening had seemed incomprehensible to her, so her response now left him hopelessly bewildered. Then, looking into her shining eyes, drinking in the most beautiful face he had ever seen, reality began slowly to dawn.

Still, he was not prepared for her next move. Circling his neck with both arms, she kissed him gently and sweetly. Then, facing a reality neither had dared to believe possible, they stood silently in front of each other, neither speaking for several moments.

Once again, it was Sara who broke the silence: "Now, Dr. Broulliette," she said slyly but with not a trace of shyness, "show me how a rabbi makes love to his lady." With that, she turned and led him by the hand to her bed. There, she learned that her rabbi did indeed understand the wisdom of life—and love.

Baraq had not arrived in Pensacola until almost 10:00 p.m., and by the time he and Sara had sated their physical desires with each other, two glorious hours had passed. As midnight arrived, they floated into a deep and satisfying sleep, their bodies locked in a warm and comfortable embrace.

Baraq, always an early riser, began drifting back to consciousness at around 5:30 but remained motionless, with Sara still nestled securely in his arms. After a moment, he reached one hand behind him and discovered Ivory curled up against the small of his back. Switching that same arm back to embrace Sara, he felt the powerful body of Lilit, who had stretched out full length in the bed on the other side of Sara; the two animals had remained lying on either side of the new lovers, keeping them locked together in the middle. The slight movement awakened Sara, who opened her eyes to find the face of Baraq directly in front of her. They exchanged their first morning kiss, and Sara whispered, "Good morning, rabbi."

Sara watched in surprise as Baraq bounded out of bed. "Where are you going?"

"I am going to bring your coffee to you in bed." It was a routine he would follow every morning thereafter.

Because Baraq scheduled all of his classes so that he taught only on Tuesdays and Thursdays, he had driven to Pensacola following regular Tuesday classes, assuming that he would return to Baton Rouge on Wednesday in time to resume his normal schedule. And Sara, knowing Baraq's schedule and the fact that he never missed class, assumed the same thing. So, she was shocked but delighted to overhear him talking on the phone to his teaching assistant: "I have been called away on personal matters," he said gravely, "and you will have to cover both classes tomorrow."

As he ended the call, he saw that Sara had been listening and blushed. "I am not capable of delivering a lecture worth hearing at the moment," he said with a wry grin, "so I thought maybe I should stay until next Monday before returning to campus."

The thought of six days alone with Baraq filled Sara with delight, but she could not resist the opportunity to bedevil him. "Don't you think you should wait until you are invited to make that decision?"

Baraq's face fell, and the proper southern gentleman replied. "I apologize, Sará. I did not mean to take too much for granted."

Once again, Sara shrieked with laughter and threw both arms around his neck. "My darling rabbi," she purred, "consider yourself formally and officially invited to stay with me forever."

Realizing he had been conned, Baraq answered in his most formal tone: "Only if you are certain, ma'am."

They were both certain, of course, and the six-day "honeymoon" flew by with a flurry of lovemaking, pillow talk, and shared thoughts of their future together. Walking into a restaurant, or simply strolling outside with Lilit, they held hands almost unconsciously, as if they had known each other all their lives. Their long talks, previously held in separate chairs that faced each other, now took place side-by-side on the couch, with Sara leaning against Baraq's muscular chest while he touched her face with a gentleness that left her feeling secure and complete. He could not overcome his amazement at the softness of her face, the warmth of her body next to his. She seemed incapable of comprehending the sheer energy with which his touch infused her very soul. Their physical coupling was matched only by the emotional bonding of two hearts that had expelled loneliness. Six days seemed a lifetime—and yet only a moment.

When Monday arrived, Baraq waited until lunch had been completed before disappearing into the bedroom to pack. Entering the room right behind him, Sara began packing as well and responded to Baraq's glance of surprise. "Hey, I'm not ever letting you get away, even for a moment." Before Baraq could tease her as she had teased him, she continued. "And yes, I consider myself formally and officially invited."

They held hands and chattered for four hours on the return trip to Baton Rouge. Then, still holding hands, they walked together into their new home and their new future.

5

To Life!

Following their first experience of awakening together in the morning, the rabbi and the widow soon realized that they had much to learn about each other. To be sure, each knew the broad outlines of the other's history, and their long hours of conversation together had included numerous details about their respective past lives. It was the discovery of little details that now amused, delighted, and bedeviled them. Sara learned that no matter how late he went to bed, Baraq invariably arose in the wee hours of the morning, and she always slept more than an hour later than he did. Even then, Baraq discovered, Sara would not, could not, converse until after her first cup of coffee. So, he learned to slip out of bed silently, retrieve the newspaper, prepare the coffee, and sit quietly reading or tapping away on his computer. Some mornings, he simply sat and watched her as she slept, his heart brimming with love. Only when she began to stir did he rise to pour the first cup exactly as she liked it, handing it to her in bed along with the newspaper and the first sweet kiss of the day.

They also had different eating schedules. Farm-grown Baraq needed to eat soon after rising, while Sara seldom took even a bite until early afternoon. So, Baraq fixed his own breakfast, and often skipped lunch, as Sara made a sandwich for herself. But they always ate a long, leisurely supper together, complete with conversations about every subject known to the human race, finding themselves in basic agreement on most subjects—politics (both were liberal), finances (both conservative), the Middle East (supportive of Israel), clothing fashions (simple, classic; hated shoes, loved sandals), the weather (both hated the cold), travel (preferably by car) ...

And sports. Here, too, they often liked or disliked the same teams and performers. They both despised whining stars who blamed others for their failures or self-centered prima donnas who thought only of personal statistics instead of team success. So when Baraq discovered that Sara was a lifelong fan of the Cardinals, he prudently kept his affection for the Cubs a secret. And when the Rams played the Saints, he tried valiantly to keep his disappointment hidden, while Sara celebrated the victory of the Rams less vigorously than was her wont. On the whole, Baraq was delighted to find a partner who loved athletics and amazed that she knew as much about baseball and football as he did. For her part, Sara was stunned to learn that a died-in-the-wool LSU fan refused to watch his beloved Tigers on television because he found it "too stressful." Whenever LSU was playing, Sara would watch and report periodic scores to Baraq, who had shut himself away in his office to write. Only when the Tigers were well in front late in a game would Baraq consent to watch the final moments of victory. When the Tigers lost, Baraq simply refused to watch. "When I watch the Tigers," he reported with a straight face, "they never lose!"

It was Baraq's work schedule that surprised Sara the most. Her former husband had left early for work in an office, traveled often, and returned home late in the evening fully spent. Baraq worked at home, writing, reading, grading papers, organizing class notes. But work he did, long hours each day. Fearing to disturb him at first, Sara soon learned that a word from her was sufficient to persuade Baraq to abandon his project of the moment, happy to chat with her instead. He insisted that he should drive her wherever she wished to go—to shop, to browse, to have her hair done—explaining that being with her was more fun than staying home alone. "Besides," he would say with feigned gruffness, "you might get lost." Because Sara's sense of direction was far better than his, they both laughed at the false explanation. Truth be told, he simply enjoyed being close to her, and she, long accustomed to doing things for herself, found that she preferred having him tag along.

"Not Now, Honey"

They also had to learn to interpret each other's moods. Baraq was almost always talkative and had a hard time understanding that sometimes Sara wanted to sit alone in total quietness. And when she was worried about something, Baraq discovered, she was grumpy with him! The first time it happened, Baraq was frantic, assuming that he had hurt or disappointed her. To his plaintive plea for an explanation, Sara had snapped: "It's not about you. I just need some alone time to think."

Bewildered, Baraq retreated to his office and waited. Several hours later, Sara appeared, once again her bright and cheerful self. She promptly launched into a detailed explanation of the problem she was facing with an insurance claim that had not been paid. She had never been angry with Baraq, she assured him, just determined to think through her problem. Thereafter, whenever Sara needed "alone time," Baraq knew that he would learn about whatever troubled her when she was ready to tell him. Reassured that Baraq was comfortable with granting her privacy made Sara less edgy, and she made an effort to inform him before she reached the boiling point.

Baraq had his "moods" too. When he decided it was time to eat, he grew irritable and impatient until fed, "a lot like a puppy," Sara noted.

When he drove in heavy traffic, Sara was utterly amazed that a thoughtless driver could induce her normally placid and proper rabbi to issue forth a stream of invectives and dark curses. "Damn," he muttered at a rude truck driver who swerved too close, "I wish I had a hand grenade to throw out the window and blast that idiot off the road." Even more amazing was the fact that Baraq seemed oblivious to the fact that his outbursts, muttered virtually inaudibly under his breath, were so out of character. Realizing that he was not actually angry made it easy for Sara to laugh at his more outlandish comments. And she was cheered by the fact that as soon as traffic eased, Baraq returned to full placidity, oblivious to his previous imprecations. She began to understand even better when, after commenting, "That fool should be home planting tomatoes instead of fouling up traffic," he admitted that his grandfather had coined the phrase.

Naps provided additional insight into both partners. Sara preferred not to sleep during the day. But when she did, Baraq knew he would not see her for two or even three hours. By contrast, Baraq napped at least once every day, often twice. "Honey, I am going to rest for a minute," he would say, and almost before Sara could respond, he was fast asleep, rising only a few minutes later refreshed and ready to resume working.

Sometimes, tiny personal habits and personality quirks undermine a relationship by causing irritation to build over time until things erupt into an angry fight. That was not the case with Baraq and Sara. They learned to laugh at each other and themselves, somehow understanding that silly idiosyncratic habits have little to do with basic character.

"Besides," Sara smiled, "at least you don't squeeze the toothpaste in the middle. That would be a deal-breaker."

Baraq responded, "Yes, I finally figured out that when you demand your infamous 'alone time,' I get some time to myself too!"

And Sara noticed that whenever she needed time to stew over a problem, Baraq often retreated to his piano. Listening to him play helped her think, and she was forced to smile more than once at his choice of songs. It really was hard to stay mad at a guy who was playing "I'm in the Mood for Love," she thought, as delicious thoughts of his affection for her accompanied the melodies he played so effortlessly.

Sara also learned to read Baraq's moods by listening to him play. "St. Louis Blues" portended a phone call to his son David, who lived there. "I'm Going to Kansas City" signaled that he was missing Nicole. When he pounded out "I'm Ready, Willing, and Able to Rock and Roll All Night," Sara knew that he was happy and feeling well. Songs like "Misty" or "The Way You Look Tonight" were an open invitation to Sara for at least a warm hug and often far more than that. More than once, Baraq's private concerts ended with a lengthy session of eager passion. For two people who were as deeply in love as they were, little stuff just did not matter.

Marriage

Only a week into their time together in Baton Rouge, Baraq raised the issue of marriage. "I don't feel right about simply living with you," he said solemnly. "We should be married."

When Sara explained that she could not risk losing the medical benefits from her former husband's company, Baraq thought for a moment and then responded with utter sincerity. "I understand that we cannot be married in a civil ceremony. But in rabbinic law, a formal betrothal is as binding as the actual marriage itself." Sara readily agreed, and Baraq composed a ceremony at which each pledged a lifelong commitment to the other, concluding with the words, "Now you are formally betrothed to me according to the traditions of Moses." To make it completely rabbinic, Baraq taught Sara the words in Hebrew! Sara's brother flew to Baton Rouge from Boston for the private ceremony, Abigail stood as witness for her father, and Sophie wept tears of joy "for both of you," she insisted.

"Are you satisfied, my darling?" Sara asked with a smile.

"Yes," said Baraq earnestly, before adding with a devilish grin, "Now, we are no longer living in sin." As had become their custom, they laughed heartily together. Thereafter, Sara noted, Baraq began wearing the wedding ring that his grandfather had once worn, "just to keep all those beautiful women out there from getting the wrong idea." But he seldom missed an opportunity to remind their friends that Sara had signed a Hebrew contract without fully understanding what she had gotten herself into. And Sara tartly responded that her brother was a brilliant Jewish lawyer who would defend her side in any disagreement, so she was not worried a bit. They also began presenting themselves to the world as husband and wife because, as Baraq explained, "In the eyes of God, we are married. So what if the state hasn't caught on yet!"

Mrs. Rabbi

En route to Lake Charles one Friday afternoon, Sara broached a subject that had begun to worry her. After two non-Jewish husbands and decades of a non-observant life, she felt that she had no idea how to be a good rabbi's wife.

Baraq was not concerned. "There is no position called 'Mrs. Rabbi,'" he assured her. "Just be Sara. Congregants with good sense will love you, and we won't worry about the others." In truth, Baraq had always marveled at how Sara interacted with his people. Her years as the wife of a corporate executive, her sensitivity to younger wives, the confidence she inspired in young children, and her skill at conversing easily with people from a wide variety of backgrounds had all prepared her to be the perfect rabbi's wife.

Her "Pied Piper" skills were demonstrated during a special service during which several small children began to grow restless, threatening to create a distraction of major proportions. Before anyone realized what was happening, Sara had acted, seating herself on the floor of the *bimah* and gathering the children around her. As she explained the meaning of the service quietly to them, charming them with her smile, the mood of the children soon matched her calm demeanor, and the service proceeded without a hitch.

At the Friday evening service the following week, Baraq asked Sara to offer the blessing for the lighting of the candles signaling the official start of Shabbat. Instead of walking directly to the front, Sara turned first toward the congregation and gestured to an older lady whom she had only recently met. Inviting the lady to join her, she explained: "Traditionally, candles are lit by a mother and her daughter together. Since my own mother cannot be here with me, I would like you to join me in reciting the blessing." Baraq knew that "Mrs. Rabbi" had scored again, charming a delighted older congregant whose own daughter lived far away and bringing warmth to a meaningful ritual that all too often was performed in a perfunctory manner.

Sara became "Mrs. Rabbi" at home too. Watching Baraq write a sermon for the first time gave Sara an unexpected insight into her new partner. She had heard several of his sermons during their first year together as friends, and she had marveled at the ease with which he delivered interesting and meaningful messages. She had always assumed that public speaking was easy for Baraq, a skill so natural that he did not have to struggle hard to succeed. She began to learn the truth when he approached her one afternoon: "Would you mind listening to this?" It was the first draft of the sermon he was planning for the following week. But in contrast to the polished masterpiece she expected, Sara was treated to what amounted to a scholarly lecture, full of facts but dry and unengaging.

When he finished reading the draft, he looked expectantly at her and asked, "Well, what do you think?" Reluctant to admit to him how boring it had sounded, Sara hesitated. "Come on, sweetie," he said. "I know it needs something, and I want you to be brutally honest with me."

Sara was both honest and brutal. "It almost put me to sleep. What in the world are you trying to say?" Undaunted, Baraq set his notes aside and began to explain his ideas to her in a normal conversational tone. When he finished, Sara simply said. "Okay. That is what you should say. But don't just read it. Say it from the heart."

"Thanks," said Baraq as he disappeared once again into his study. Three drafts later, Sara was finally satisfied. When he delivered the sermon the following week, several members of the congregation dubbed it one of his best messages ever. En route to their room after service, Baraq was ecstatic. "Boy, are you going to make me a better rabbi!"

Sara never hesitated to share her opinions frankly after that, and Baraq's sermons continued to improve. Soon, like an adoring puppy eager to be petted, Baraq routinely brought draft after draft to Sara, studying her face for clues as he watched her read. Her criticism never discouraged him but simply sent him back to his keyboard time and again. He remained confident that the end product was worth the effort.

A similar result flowed from their first hospital visit together. At the bedside of a congregant facing a difficult operation on the morrow, Baraq was strong and resolute, offering just the right mix of encouragement and concern to the anxious patient and her family. But he was utterly rabbinic, formal, proper, and almost detached. Just as he was ready to end the visit by offering a special prayer for healing, Sara nudged Baraq aside and sat on the edge of the bed. Taking one of the patient's hands in both of hers, she began to speak softly. "I know this is difficult for you. And I am grateful that you have such a supportive family at your side. From what I hear, the woman scheduled to do your operation is the best surgeon in the area. So I believe that when this is over, you will be amazed at how much better you feel."

Baraq saw firsthand the warm heart of his beloved, and he also noticed the palpable change in the countenance of the patient. The young woman who had battled illness herself knew as much as he did about lengthy operations, and she had found exactly the right words. Silently, he breathed a prayer of thanks to God for her presence in that sick room.

Mrs. Professor

Sara was also surprised at the intensive preparation Baraq made for his university classes. Once, when she knew he was battling a nasty cold, she suggested that he rest rather than worry about having every detail fully prepared for the lecture on the following day. "You know the subject inside and out," she noted. "No one would know if you winged it just this once."

"I would know," said Baraq quietly, and Sara gave up the battle.

Because she enjoyed attending class with Baraq, Sara also discovered a lot about his professorial side and was amazed at the ways in which he handled various classroom situations. Without fail, he demanded that his students match his ardor for the subject with hard work and preparation, and he was merciless whenever a student admitted that an assignment had been left undone. More than once, he ordered that those who had not completed the assigned reading leave the room. "I am not going to waste my time explaining concepts that you are unprepared to grasp," he would say testily. "So, sit in the hall until you finish the reading, and don't come tomorrow unless you are ready to learn."

Asked how to prepare for a test on the morrow, students were treated to a classic Baraq-ism: "A word to the wise, and I am sorry to exclude so many of you," before hearing his simple formula: "Read the book, review your notes, get plenty of sleep, and don't make stupid mistakes on your answer sheet." Returning a test on which the scores were exceptionally low, Baraq snapped, "The entire class has the same illness—low grade fever!"

Then, there was the student who, receiving a low grade on a term paper, asked for permission to write a second paper and thereby earn a higher grade. "Look," growled Dr. Broulliette, "if I have to read two 'C' papers rather than one, your grade will go down. I am looking for quality rather than quantity."

Sensing that the student did not understand his reasoning, Baraq uttered an explanation that soon became famous among his students. "Quality is like buying oats, young lady," he noted. "If you want nice fresh oats, you have to be willing to pay a fair price for them. However, if you can be happy with oats that have already been through the horse once, they cost a lot less." Even to students who had never set foot on a farm, Baraq's meaning was clear. The student finally understood that one quality research paper was worth more than two mediocre ones.

"Truth be told," a student once confessed to Sara, "your husband is the hardest professor I have ever had. But he is also the best lecturer I have ever heard, and he is fair, so I have really learned a lot." He then added plaintively, "Even though my grade does not reflect it."

Baraq also earned the reputation for compassion whenever a student ran into difficulty. He was readily available for conferences with troubled students, and he offered extra tutoring to anyone who demonstrated a willingness to try hard. He refused to penalize students for illness, and he was generous in allowing extensions for assignments or make-up tests. But it was handicapped students who captured Baraq's heart, and he insisted that they be seated in the front of the class so that he could pay special attention to them. Lilit was a major ally in this regard. She had become accustomed to a wheelchair when Baraq's mom had been confined during the final year of her life, and she seemed to assume that anyone so confined was special, family. So, she spent many a class settled close to any student in a wheelchair, resting her giant head as close to the occupant as she could. Because of his gentle acceptance of these "special" kids, Baraq was asked to serve as the faculty advisor for the Special Needs Club. "Ah, they think I am handicapped because I am old," he groused, but he never missed a meeting or special event and became a passionate advocate for Americans with disabilities.

The most unusual aspect of Baraq's teaching involved his brand of humor. Once, asked why Jews practice circumcision, Baraq quipped: "Because Jewish women can't resist anything that is 15 percent off!" before launching into a detailed survey of the historical, cultural, and theological foundation of the custom. When a pre-med major, ignoring the cultural importance of the practice in traditional Judaism, argued that circumcision was medically unnecessary and painful, Baraq seemed to agree readily. "In fact," he admitted, "I could not walk for months after it was done to me." It took a moment for the class to recognize that Baraq, who had been only eight days old when he was circumcised, as are all Jewish boys, was offering a ridiculous response to a question he felt improper.

Televangelists were the objects of Baraq's harshest criticism, underscored dramatically by the unforgettable, humorous package in which he wrapped it. During a lecture about the ways in which biblical prophets responded to what they perceived to be the presence of God, Baraq offered this compelling comparison. "The God who appeared to these men inspired such awe that they often fell to their faces in full consciousness of their own unworthiness and sin," he began. By contrast, "Obviously, the modern wannabe counterparts of the true prophet, the televangelists who come prancing across the sound stage wearing their $2,000 sharkskin suits and their bouffant hairdos, are talking to a different deity but surely not the biblical Sovereign of the universe." He then noted sarcastically that the message received by money-grubbing televangelists was invariably the same: "Give your souls to Jesus ... but send your money to me!"

Biblical prophets, he had continued, were brokenhearted at the thought of impending punishment soon to be visited on their hearers, again quite unlike "these modern fools who are just too damn happy to announce that everyone is going to hell except them."

When the largest television station in the city invited Baraq to appear on a weekly Sunday morning program, he accepted, only to discover when he and Sara arrived at the Wednesday afternoon taping that a nationally prominent televangelist, who was in town for a crusade at a local church, had been slated for the same program. The local station manager, aware of their sharp differences, was determined to stage a debate between the two men.

When the eager manager disclosed his plan for the debate, Baraq attempted to back out and stood to leave. Then, the man whom he had often criticized made a critical error. "What's the matter, *doctor*?" he asked bitingly. "Are you afraid to face the truth?"

Sara watched with a mixture of trepidation and anticipation as Baraq turned slowly and responded. "If I thought you could recognize or acknowledge the truth, I would be utterly amazed." The debate was on.

Things started slowly as Baraq and the televangelist each made brief opening comments about their respective backgrounds and visions of religious faith. But the moderator quickly changed the tone. "Reverend," he asked with mock sincerity, "You have stated publicly your view that there is only one way to find God, and that is through acceptance of Jesus as you perceive him. If that is in fact your position, could you explain your thinking to our viewers?"

The televangelist, who had been ordained after a brief apprenticeship with a small, local fundamentalist church but had no formal theological training, began his answer with obvious relish. "God says," he began grandiloquently while brandishing his Bible vigorously, "'I [Jesus] am the way.' Not *a* way, you understand, *the* way, the *only* way. But that is not all. Jesus also said, 'No man comes to the Father except through me.'" Then, he added the clincher. "The Bible said it, I believe it, and that settles it."

Sara watched as the moderator asked Baraq,. "Dr. Broulliette, how do you respond?" She was not surprised at his answer.

"Well, in fact, that question is asked in Jewish liturgy: 'Where can we find You?' The very next sentence provides the Jewish answer: 'You are as close to us as breathing, yet You are farther than the farthermost star.' In other words, we don't find God, because God is not lost. *God finds us*. And this is a point made early in Genesis when we humans committed our initial act of disobedience. If religion were all about finding God, we would expect to find Adam and Eve, having just experienced the pain of disobedience for the first time, thrashing around in the garden looking frantically for God. But that is not the story. Not only were they not searching for God, they hid themselves in shame and were frightened when they actually did come into his presence."

As the televangelist and the moderator stared at Baraq with mouths gaping open, Baraq continued.

"In short, according to Genesis, God was not the one hiding. To the contrary, God came looking for Adam and Eve. He was the one asking: 'Where are you?'"

"This theme is so pervasive in Judaism," Baraq added, warming to the task, "that one of the greatest Jewish scholars of the twentieth century, Abraham Joshua Heschel, wrote a powerful book titled *God in Search of Man.* The point is clear. No one knows how to find God. We humans simply do not have that ability. All arrogant claims to the contrary, we can only deceive ourselves if we announce that we can find God. What is more, the Genesis story clearly implies something even more compelling. Most of the time, our sinfulness makes us want to *avoid* contact with God."

Still Baraq was not finished. "Here is the response of Judaism to a great human conundrum. When we hear the claim that 'no one comes to God except' through our group or by following our theology, we simply smile, because we know we have just heard the answer to a question that is illegitimate. As Jews, we are not looking for the magic path to God. Long ago, God found Adam and Eve in the Garden of Eden, found Moses on the backside of the desert, found us all bound by the shackles of Egyptian slavery. Whether we wish it to be true or not, wherever we are, God is there."

Baraq then quoted from what Sara recognized as one of his favorite psalms, explaining, "Here is how one of our greatest poets expressed it:

Where can I go away from Your spirit?
Where can I flee from Your presence?
If I rise up to heaven, You are there.

If I go down into hell, You are there also.
If I take wings with the dawn and alight on the western
horizon,
even there Your hand will be guiding me,
Your right hand will be holding me fast.
If I say, 'Surely darkness will conceal me,
night will provide me with cover,'
Darkness is not dark for You;
night is as light as day, they are both the same."

Baraq finally finished with a flourish. "So, you see, the problem is not finding God but deciding how we will react when God finds us."

To the angry protest of the reverend, "But the Bible says …" Baraq had a simple response. "You cannot detach a single statement from its context and take everything in the Bible literally."

At once the televangelist seized the opening. "It is obvious that you don't believe the Bible, *doctor*," he retorted, his voice once again dripping with acidic sarcasm. "God says what he means and means what he says. Not even you can find a way around that."

Baraq was unfazed. "So you believe that everything in the Bible is literally true? Nothing is metaphorical?" Sara knew Baraq well enough to realize that he was angry but not with the heated anger that clouds the mind. His was the cold fury that helped him focus precisely on his target. And she knew what was coming next.

"I'll repeat, *doctor*, so that even you can understand if you are open-minded. God says what he means and means what he says."

Baraq smiled and waited silently for the moderator to speak. "Dr. Broulliette, again, how do you respond?"

"I'll ask a specific question if I may. Reverend, when Genesis tells us that the wife of Lot was turned into 'a block of salt' for the act of taking a final glance at her burning home, does that mean that she became a pile of sodium chloride?"

"It means exactly that," responded the preacher.

"I see," said Baraq, as he appeared to search for just the right way to continue. "So, when Jesus tells his disciples that they are 'the salt of the earth,' were they, too, sodium chloride?"

The now furious preached literally shouted. "That is an obvious metaphor."

"Obvious to you, perhaps," said Baraq. "But that one I prefer to believe is literal."

At this point, the televangelist angrily accused Baraq of "disrespecting our Lord."

"Not at all," declared Baraq, his tone still resolute and measured. "I have great respect for Jesus. After all," and now Baraq was being Baraq, "he was one of our boys."

By now, the moderator was twisting his hands in his lap as he waited for Baraq's parting thrust at the hapless minister. "I'm glad you have admitted on television that you believe *some* parts of the Bible are metaphorical rather than strictly literal. Your only problem is that you and I disagree on which parts they are."

The moderator, struggling to regain his composure, consulted his notes and changed the subject. "Let's move on." Turning again to the televangelist, he spoke: "Reverend, you are on record as opposing the ordination of women. Would you share your reasoning with our audience?"

The minister was more than anxious to reply. "We are the church of Jesus Christ," he thundered. "And we follow his example without question. Since he chose only men to be his apostles, we do the same thing."

Without waiting for the moderator, Baraq responded. "That is the silliest explanation I have ever heard."

"You only think that because you have no respect for Jesus," the minister retorted, retreating once more to his favorite accusation of anyone who disagreed with him.

"No," said Baraq. "Your premise is silly because Jesus chose only *Jews* to be his apostles. And you certainly do not follow *that* example."

The minister had had enough. He sprang to his feet, ripped the microphone from his lapel, and began to stalk out of the room. At the door, he whirled and shouted, "This stupid episode will never air. My lawyers will make certain of that." With that, he was gone.

"Well, at least he and I agree on one thing," Baraq remarked to the moderator, and he, too, rose to leave.

The minister got his wish, and the station prudently decided not to run the piece.

Driving home from the station, Sara asked Baraq gently, "Honey, do you think you came on a bit too strong?"

"No," said Baraq, and Sara noticed how white his knuckles were as he gripped the steering wheel. "I hate it when I am accused of disrespecting Jesus. Truthfully, he had a lot of good ideas, and I don't know anything bad about him. But I hate it even more when one of his so-called followers perverts his message. There is absolutely nothing loving about a preacher screaming that anyone who disagrees with him is slated for eternal torment."

Sara thought it wise to change the subject.

Abigail

Baraq's adopted daughter Abigail had been living with him in Baton Rouge throughout the first year of friendship between Sara and Baraq. Once Sara arrived in the home, she was determined to reach the young girl, taking her shopping, helping with her schoolwork, and spending long hours exchanging "girl talk." She learned to her delight that Abigail, whose biological mother lived far away in Virginia, was willing to open her heart to her and accept her as a friend and ally. On her part, Sara could not evade the thought that Abigail was exactly the daughter she had always longed for.

As Abigail approached high school graduation, Sara chatted with her about her grades and was shocked to hear the younger girl's attitude. "I don't want to know about the things they insist on teaching in school," she admitted, "because they won't help me do what I have always known I want to do."

"And what is that?" asked Sara.

"Aw, I can't tell you because Dad thinks it's dumb."

"But, Abigail, have you ever actually told your father what you want to do after high school?"

When the girl admitted that she had never actually explained to Baraq why she disdained school and had dreams of a life unrelated to academia, Sara insisted that he needed to know what was on his daughter's mind. "Besides," she told Abigail, "Your father may surprise you. I know he is terribly worried about you and sometimes feels that he has failed you because you have done so poorly in school. Learning that you have an ambitious plan for your future may be something he will welcome."

"But he won't like it because he thinks everyone should go to college."

"It is unfair to assume that your father will refuse to accept something you truly long to do with your life. Give him a chance."

When Abigail reluctantly agreed to reveal her secret to her father, she insisted that Sara be at her side. "I know he won't get mad at me if you are there," she said, "because he loves you."

"Abigail, there is no way you can imagine how much your father truly loves you as well." Even though she could not break her promise not to alert Baraq to Abigail's impending announcement, whatever it might be, Sara was certain that Baraq would handle whatever Abigail revealed to him. Still, she was shocked at the short speech the young girl made to her father after supper the following evening. With the abrupt directness of a modern teen, it went something like this.

"Hey, Dad, I know you think I am irresponsible and immature because I have not even tried to do well in school. But here's the thing. School has nothing to do with what I want out of life. Now, before you react, let me remind you of something. Do you remember how I loved to trim your beard for you even when I was a small girl of seven or eight?"

As Baraq nodded, Abigail plunged ahead. "Even then, you knew I was really good with those scissors and would make your beard look great. You trusted me. Well, I knew that I wanted to make people, not just you, look good. And that is what I want to do now. I want to go to a school of cosmetology and learn how to do cool haircuts, coloration, eyebrows, nails, makeup, wardrobe, etc. See, I won't be just a beautician. I'll be well-trained enough to actually help people with the whole process of looking good. So, what do you think? I'm not really interested in college, you know."

As Abigail paused to breathe, both she and Sara scanned the impassive face of Baraq —the university professor, the rabbi—but more than anything, the loving father. As he often did, Baraq took a moment to collect his thoughts before responding. "OK, Abbey. If that is what you want to do, then I have only this to say: let's find the best school available so you can become the best damned beauty consultant in the world. But you must make a total commitment and refuse to let anything deter you from your goal."

Sara smiled to herself. Abigail breathed a sigh of relief and rushed to embrace her father. "Will you really help me?"

"Help you? I plan to be your first client. You surely don't know anyone who needs more help to look good than me!"

With less than a semester remaining in her high school years, feeling that the pressure to be an academic whiz had been removed, Abigail surprised everyone with the best grades she had ever earned in school. She also went through the interview process required to enroll in the prestigious Paul Mitchell School, and Sara was gratified at the relaxed way she began to relate once again with her father.

Still, Sara was not surprised that Baraq continued to worry about his beautiful daughter. "I hope I am doing the correct thing," he confided to Sara. "I never dreamed she would not go to college, much less that she would choose such a career. I console myself by remembering that the final refuge of a righteous man is his own integrity, and I know I have done my best. Perhaps someday, Abigail will discover how much I truly love her." Although he appeared to speak calmly, the silver tears trickling down his rugged cheeks betrayed the depth of his emotions.

A Few Small Changes

Understanding that Baraq was careful with his money and that he earned only a modest income, Sara was nervous about broaching the subject of the house. Although she longed to remodel it completely, Baraq seemed not to notice that it was in terrible condition. She decided to start slowly. "Honey, I have a few dollars saved. Would you mind terribly if I made a few small changes around the house?"

Baraq agreed, failing to ask what "small changes" Sara had in mind. They moved into the tiny garage apartment in the back of the main house, and they left the next morning on a two-week trip to St. Louis and Kansas City, where Sara would meet Baraq's two older children for the first time. It was a moment that she dreaded. Because of her experiences with Michael's children, it was only natural that Sara felt apprehensive about her first meeting with David and Nicole. She need not have worried. The trip was an unqualified success. In St. Louis, David embraced Sara with a simple greeting: "Hi, Mom," accepting her at first sight. Nicole in Kansas City was more expressive. "Thanks for giving me my old dad back," she told Sara, who was relieved and gratified that both children recognized the great love she bore for their father.

She also met Thomas, Baraq's grandson. It was love at first sight. The eight-year old, struggling to choose the correct way to address her, began to call her "Triple G," and Sara had no idea what he meant. When Thomas explained that "Triple G" was a superhero, everyone knew that Sara had earned an unqualified "A" on the toughest test of all.

After David arrived from St. Louis, the five Broulliettes spent two glorious weeks together in Kansas City. They swam, biked, ate at a variety of restaurants, and attended an outdoor concert at the famous Starlight Theater. Watching Baraq with his children, Sara loved him even more. She was amazed at the concern they showed for his health and at the details of their lives they shared readily with him. And she was certain that any man who maintained such a close relationship with his children could surely love her for a lifetime. On the drive home, they chattered endlessly about future family trips, including Sara's dream of a family cruise. Maybe, Sara dared to think silently, I can become a mother after all.

Still, as she reflected on the reception Baraq's children had granted her, Sara could not help but remember the bitterness of her experience with her previous two stepchildren. Their rebuff had broken her heart, and she was reluctant to make herself susceptible to heartbreak once again at the hands of David, Nicole, and Abigail. But she could not deny the differences between the two sets of stepchildren. Whereas Michael had given his children far more materially than Baraq's modest resources had made possible, they had been denied the time and attention of their father, whereas Baraq's children had remained the center of his focus in spite of his demanding schedule. Now, it seemed that the results of these two parental approaches were becoming apparent. Not only did Baraq's children adore their father. They were obviously ready to accept his new partner with open hearts, grateful that her presence in his life would ease the loneliness they knew he had endured. As her fears about Michael's children had proved correct, so now Sara dared to believe that her hopes for a loving relationship with Baraq's son and daughters could come to fruition. She was right both times.

Returning from their visit, Baraq entered his house and was totally shocked. He had imagined a little paint, fresh carpet, and perhaps a new fixture or two. Instead, he stood gazing at a house that was completely gutted. All the furniture had been moved to a storage facility, walls and ceilings had been stripped of sheetrock and stood with studs bare, the floors were devoid of covering, and he walked on bare concrete. The wall between two smaller bedrooms had been completely removed to create one large room, and plumbers had jackhammered the concrete foundation in the bathrooms so that toilets, vanities, tubs, and showers could be repositioned. All the old fixtures and appliances were gone.

"Small changes indeed!" But Baraq had agreed and prudently kept his thoughts to himself.

The remodeling revealed another side of Sara. Acting as her own general contractor, she planned every tiny detail, ordered materials, dealt firmly with workers, and plotted the progress of each day. When an incompetent workman needed to be fired, Sara proved capable of that task as well, even though her ex-boxer mate insisted that he and Lilit stand at her side when she delivered the message. "Your work is not satisfactory. Please gather your tools, turn in the hours that you have worked so far, and vacate the property at once." Baraq hoped she would never have to fire him!

And Baraq saw an expert negotiator at work as well. Waiting for a plumber to arrive one morning, Sara confided to Baraq that she expected to pay about $4,000 for the job on which he was offering a bid. When the plumber offered an opening bid of $3,750, Baraq was prepared to accept immediately, but a raised eyebrow from Sara warned him to hold his peace.

"How close am I?" the plumber asked. Sara frowned and seemed to be deep in thought. Both Baraq and the plumber shifted nervously at her protracted silence.

"Well," she finally answered, "we are very close." After another uncomfortable pause, she asked, "Is that the absolute best price?"

Now it was the plumber's turn to frown. "I really cannot go any lower than $3,550" was his response.

Again, Sara paused while Baraq fidgeted. "If that is your best price, we have a deal," she said finally, extending her hand.

When they were alone, and Baraq questioned her, Sara said simply, "I told him the truth. We *were* close to a deal at his opening number. And if that had been his lowest bid, I would have been happy. But I told him before he arrived that I wanted his best price, so I wanted to make sure I got it."

Throughout the six-month project, Baraq took a back seat to Sara, honoring her judgment. He became the official "gofer," trotting off to the lumber yard or paint store when supplies were needed, making certain that he brought home exactly what she had ordered. For it was Sara who chose the tile, selected the perfect tint for each coat of paint, and agreed to fixtures, cabinets, and hardware only when they met her demanding standards.

When the house was completed, Baraq's faith in Sara's abilities was rewarded. The new living quarters were beautiful, and Baraq spotted not a single change that he would have made. "Elegant but not ostentatious," mused Baraq. A lot like the designer herself! In the meantime, Sara's home in Pensacola finally sold, easing her financial burden and closing that chapter of her life. Her car was adorned with a "Geaux Tigers" bumper sticker. Baton Rouge was home.

The New Home

Baraq loved the new home Sara had created. In truth, it was by far the nicest place in which he had ever lived. As a student, he had occupied a succession of tiny apartments complete with mismatched secondhand furniture, threadbare carpet, and dingy walls. In Israel, the small home of his host family had been immaculate but cramped. Even during his first marriage, his wife and he had been able to afford only a small apartment before buying their first home together. It, too, was tiny, with three small bedrooms and a single bathroom. When David and Nicole arrived, there was scarcely room to breathe. After his illness, he had purchased the house in Baton Rouge that Sara saw in such poor condition. Baraq either did not notice or did not care about things like leaky faucets, small cracks in the walls, or burned-out light fixtures. But he discovered that he enjoyed nice things: appliances that worked properly, furniture that matched, pictures and decorations that were carefully chosen and tastefully displayed, and especially a gleaming new kitchen where he could cook to his heart's content.

Sara was also delighted with the new place, her enjoyment enhanced by the obvious joy it brought to Baraq. When Baraq converted the garage apartment into a private studio just for her, giving her a perfect place in which to resume her craftwork as well as a haven in which to spend her "alone time," she was ecstatic. When it turned out that she could hear Baraq's piano renditions even in the studio, her joy was complete.

Growing Old Together

Given the age and medical history of both partners, it was inevitable that health should become a concern. Although they usually went everywhere together, Baraq thought little about it when Sara declined to accompany him one evening to a lecture. "I don't feel well" was all she had said. When he returned home at 10:00 p.m., Baraq discovered that his betrothed was running a raging temperature of almost 103 degrees. Sara assured him that she would be okay until morning, but Baraq insisted that she needed medical help at once. Grabbing the phone, he called the old friend whose advice had sent him to the hospital on the morning of his heart attack and explained the situation to him. Handing the phone to Sara, he instructed her to describe her situation to the doctor.

After a brief chat, Dr. Goldman asked to speak once again with Baraq. Sara heard him say, "I'll be right there," and then, he bolted out the door.

Over two hours later, he returned, medications in hand. He had gone to the doctor's home on the far side of town to obtain the proper prescriptions and then had driven back to the other side of Baton Rouge to find a twenty-four-hour pharmacy. There he waited until past midnight for the prescriptions to be filled and rushed back to the side of his beloved. Dispensing the medicine, rearranging her pillows, straightening the bed covers, he hovered over Sara like a nervous mother hen until she slipped mercifully to sleep. When she awakened, feeling markedly better, the first thing she saw was Baraq, still seated in the chair beside her bed, a book askew in his lap, his chin nodding down to his chest. He had been there through the night, "just in case you needed me."

Sara's turn to care for Baraq came only a few weeks later. He had not suffered a seizure in months and never in Sara's presence. Startled awake early one morning by the excited barking of Lilit, she rushed into Baraq's office, where he was lying prone, the faithful dog pawing at his chest frantically. Only a minute passed before Baraq regained consciousness and admitted sheepishly that Lilit had warned him well in advance of his fall. "I thought I could make it to the bed in time," he said. "I just wanted to finish the chapter I was writing before I closed my computer program."

Ignoring his protests, Sara ordered an ambulance to rush Baraq to the emergency room, where it was her turn to sit at his side throughout the day while a battery of tests confirmed that Baraq had not suffered a heart attack. "Only a little seizure," he said lamely. On the drive home from the hospital, Sara also admitted to Baraq what she had done. During her ordeal, Sara said, she had felt quite ill all day long but had not wanted to worry her husband. Because she was determined to accompany Baraq to the lecture, she had not told him of her problem until the last minute.

"We could have had you medicated much earlier if you had told me the truth," Baraq fussed.

"Of course, you are the one to talk," Sara shot back. "You ignored the warning of your service dog, the girl who has never been wrong in eight years, trying to be a hero. And just so you know, finding you prostrate on the floor was not much fun."

As they talked, both realized how alone they had been all of their lives. Sara's first husband had turned his back on her during her terrible ordeal, and even her beloved Michael, the former Navy officer and college athlete, had often left her to fend for herself whenever she had been ill. Baraq had faced his illness alone as well, driving himself to endless visits at the hospital, rehabilitation clinics, and post-attack checkups at the cardiologist's office. When they had first learned of each other's history, he had grieved at the thought of a partner leaving Sara on her own, and she had found unfathomable the idea of him driving himself all over town seeking medical treatment.

That day they made a solemn pledge that neither would withhold even minor aches and pains from the other. "No more 'tough guy' stuff for either of us," they agreed. "When one of us is sick, we go through it together."

Spicing Up Life

LSU provided another aspect to the life of Baraq and Sara. The huge university offered a play, a concert, or an interesting lecture virtually every night of the week. And given the eclectic tastes of both partners, they were never hard pressed to find something interesting to do. After her years in the restricted enclave of Pensacola, Sara was delighted at the opportunity to expand her cultural tastes. For his part, Baraq had never been comfortable attending functions alone. With Sara at his side, he, too, embraced this exciting aspect of university life.

As promised by Baraq, the growing city of Baton Rouge proved to be an interesting place as well. The "Little Theater" regularly presented excellent plays, and the city symphony, able to draw from music professors and top students at LSU and Southern University, was totally professional. Since both partners appreciated a wide range of music, the annual jazz fest brought them both as much joy as the classical presentations of the symphony. On the one hand, watching Baraq tap his feet to the jazz rhythm of a local ensemble seemed to belie his serious mien. But Sara also recalled the opera "Elijah" that they had shared together, especially the moment when the voice of the tenor soloist had soared with the words, "If with all your heart ye truly seek me, ye shall ever surely find me. Thus saith our God." Seeing warm tears course down Baraq's cheeks at the words, Sara believed that in finding each other, they truly had found God as well. Or, as Baraq phrased the matter, "God found us for each other."

In addition to entertaining performances by guest artists and students, LSU also offered a wide variety of adult education or self-improvement courses. Sara enrolled in a yoga class, Baraq signed up for woodworking, and they joined a jitterbug dance class together. Everything they did brought them closer together, increasing their mutual admiration for each other and ratifying the decision they had made to share each other's lives.

By far, the most intriguing social outlet in town was the local riverboat casino, which, Baraq learned, featured hundreds of slot machines, a favorite pastime of Sara. They went only infrequently, and she never risked much but could spend an hour or two at the slots just for the fun of watching the tumblers as they fell, once in a while, into perfect alignment. Over time, she became convinced that a quick rub of Baraq's bald pate held the key to luck and winning. When Baraq grudgingly agreed to pull a lever or two, he promptly won almost $300, and Sara's conviction that rabbis really do have a direct line to a higher power was confirmed. Truth be told, they never won or lost more than a few dollars. The simple experience of dazzling lights illuminating a crowd of players who alternately groaned or cheered provided the true reason for their visits. And the casino had three first-class restaurants.

"The" Miracle

All in all, the lives of Baraq and Sara appeared to have become a series of tiny miracles that, taken together, had yielded the greatest blessing of all. Often, they lay in bed together recalling the early moments of their relationship. What if Sara had met someone really cool on her website? Or Baraq on his? What if Isaac had not suggested Aunt Sophie? What if Michael had lived, or Abigail's mother had stayed? What if Lilit had not persisted in warning Baraq about his impending heart attack? If he had not called Dr. Goldman? If the ambulance had been delayed? What if Sara had sold her house quickly and moved to Atlanta before they could meet?

Late one evening, Baraq looked at the issue another way. "I wish I had met you when we were kids," he said wistfully. "It would have been wonderful to love only you all of my life."

"No, Baraq," Sara responded reflectively. "We became who we are now only because of all the things we suffered, all the loves we held and lost, all the disappointments, all the false starts and unrealistic hopes of youth and immaturity."

Baraq knew she was correct. "Besides," she continued, "We did not have enough sense to love each other when we were young. It was necessary for us to acquire a bit of wisdom before we could recognize the truth about ourselves and understand the value of real love."

Although he was a rabbi, Baraq's personal view of God would have surprised some people. He thought it foolish to believe that a giant cosmic Santa Claus somewhere in the heavens would take the time to become involved in the daily grind of an individual life. For him, "God" was a word that symbolized the cosmic totality of the impulse for goodness that lies in the heart of every human being in the universe. Since he knew it would be impossible to repeat this full definition whenever he spoke of spiritual matters, he continued to use "God" as a matter of convenience. But he was personally more comfortable with the word "godness," which he thought more accurate than a word that implied a Person.

His relationship with Sara caused him to question some of his assumptions for the first time. For her part, Sara was convinced that angels had personally and carefully plotted the course of their lives, finally bringing them together at exactly the perfect moment. "Our union is a miracle," she insisted. "That's my story, and I'm sticking to it."

The more he thought about it, the harder it was for Baraq to propose a better interpretation.

Lying side by side one evening, drifting toward peaceful sleep, Baraq began to sing softly. Sara had learned the special blessing as a child, and she knew its tune and words by heart. Although she did not understand the meaning of the Hebrew words, Sara quietly added her voice to his:

> *"Barukh 'atta, 'Adonai, 'Eloheinu melekh ha-'olam,*
> *She he-Hiyanu, ve-qiyemanu,*
> *ve-higi'anu la-zeman ha-zeh."*

"What do the words mean, bear bear?" She was nestled close to his chest, their two hearts beating as one. As he translated for her, Baraq discovered new meaning for his own life in the familiar, ancient words.

"Blessed art Thou, O Lord our God, King of the universe,
You have kept us alive, You have strengthened us,
And You have brought us to this moment in time."

"This moment," he whispered to himself, as Sara drifted into peaceful slumber. "I am not alone anymore." Finally, Baraq realized, he had found what God had promised Adam. As Sara slept once again in his arms, he recalled the story of the first man. As the ancient narrative phrased it, God had looked back at the end of each of the six days of creation, checking his handiwork and declaring it to be "good." And Baraq thought about his earlier uneasiness over the fact that his aloneness, like that of Adam, had seemed to be the one part of divine creation that God had declared "*not* good." He also knew that in the Genesis story, even under the guiding hand of the divine, the search for Adam's perfect mate had taken a long time, requiring Adam to examine every animal in the world until he learned that no other creature was perfect for him. Only then had God created the one special someone named Eve to be Adam's *'ezer ke-negdo*.

Now, after his own long years of loneliness, Baraq finally understood, God had created his one special someone, too, his *'ezer ke-negdo*, lovely Sara, his "full and equal partner."

Postlude

The story you have just read is about a rabbi from Louisiana and a widow who was living in Florida when they met. And I admit it is a bit hard to believe that it actually happened the way Jeff, Carlita, and I presented it. But I assure you that it did. Since Dr. Broulliette had previously lived and worked in several other states as well as in Europe and the Middle East, it was difficult to get the facts of his life straight. Because Sara had lived at one time or another in Illinois, Louisiana, Tennessee, California, and Georgia before settling in Florida, her steps were not easy to retrace, either. That is why it took three of us to collaborate on the finished product.

As he explained in the first chapter, Dr. Broulliette's student Jeff did the research for the first part and also benefitted from several conversations he had with the rabbi, although he never revealed his intention to write about him. The second part, as you saw, was written by Sara's maid and girl Friday in Florida, Carlita, who became her confidant following the death of her husband and mother. But I am the only one who was actually present to witness everything that happened once the two met, so I was the logical one to bring the story to its conclusion from that point on.

Because Jeff was well educated, he was able to write Chapter One by himself. Carlita, as you remember, was not a native speaker of English, so Jeff had to help her translate her Spanish notes before she could complete her contribution.

My problem was even more difficult to solve. You see, my native language is not English either; it's … well, "dog." But since I was the only one who was always present both in Baton Rouge and in Pensacola, there was just no one else available who could get the facts straight.

Now, I know what you're thinking. A dog? Yes, my paws are too big for those ridiculous little keyboards, and I confess that I was unable to type my own thoughts. On the other hand, I have attended college with Dr. Broulliette for many years, studied for my "bark" mitzvah, and listened carefully to many an erudite lecture. And as anyone who understands animals realizes, dogs (and cats, too, Ivory reminds me) just know stuff that people cannot imagine.

Take for example the time that Dr. Broulliette was about to have his heart attack. I could hear his heart beating irregularly, I smelled the chemical changes taking place in his body, and I knew exactly what was happening, but he didn't even realize he needed help. In fact, he thought I had forgotten my training or was being disobedient, and I had to get tough just to convince him to call his doctor and get sound medical advice.

And of course I knew he and Sara were in love with each other long before either of them admitted it to themselves. Ivory knew it, too, and we spent many an hour trying to figure out how to get them to understand what was happening to them both. You see, humans talk a lot, but they don't actually *communicate* very well. Ivory and I can't talk, so we actually have to pay attention to each other, and that works better most of the time. In the case of Sara and Baraq, Ivory and I intuited the "love" angle a lot quicker than the two humans did.

One of the things Ivory and I discussed (okay, "communicated" to each other) was how nervous we both were when our two humans took their first steps back into the world of dating. Ivory didn't like any of Sara's first dates and tried so hard to show her how she felt that the poor soul came to believe her loving cat was leery of everybody. That is what made it so easy for Ivory to show Sara how much she loved Dr. Broulliette without using any words. We both laughed about that.

As for me, I listened to Dr. Broulliette's conversations with the ladies he met by phone and have never been so bored. And that one date he had in New Orleans was the worst. I mean, the woman was just not right for him. So when Sara came into the picture, all I had to do was cozy up to her, and the difference was finally apparent even to Dr. Broulliette. I'm glad he followed my advice on this one.

Of course, Ivory really does love Dr. Broulliette, and I fell for Sara the first time we met. Things might have progressed more quickly if they both had been as discerning as Ivory and I were, but you know humans. And the story might not have been as interesting anyway. Now, I admit that I was really angry with Dr. Broulliette when I thought he had broken Sara's heart. I know I should not have left him alone when he went to bed, but I was more concerned about Sara at the moment, and I just knew Ivory would stare some sense into the man.

But there was still the problem of telling the story. Fortunately, I can communicate nonverbally because I am a very special kind of dog. You see, the good Lord knew that Dr. Broulliette needed help and knew also that he was too hard-headed to believe in guardian angels just because he says he has never seen one. But he does truly love dogs, so the plan was to have me inhabit the body of a Bullmastiff and come into Dr.

Broulliette's life as his protector. And *that* he accepted without a second thought. Scholars are so predictable!

Anyway, with my help, the man's life finally took a turn for the better, as I believe you can now agree, and I thought people ought to know about it. After I thought about it for a while, I realized that getting the story out wouldn't really be all that difficult. With divine permission, I sprinkled a little angel dust on Dr. Broulliette's keyboard, blinked twice, and transported the story of *The Rabbi and the Widow* to a folder in "My Documents" where I knew he would eventually find it. It took a while, but he finally came across it during a periodic updating of his files one day.

I had to laugh when he read it for the first time, because he was quite unable to remember having written it. At first, of course, he assumed that Sara must have been responsible, but when she denied any knowledge of it as well, they had to admit that its appearance was a mystery. So, they read the story together and learned for the first time about the private thoughts they had been reluctant to reveal to each other. They alternately blushed and giggled a lot, but they realized that the story was true, and that's when they agreed that maybe other people facing hard times might find inspiration by reading how their lives had turned out.

Dr. Broulliette sent a copy of the manuscript to a colleague at LSU who was a professor of literature, she contacted a publisher friend, and the publisher decided a lot of people needing a little encouragement would buy the book. I'm glad the publisher was correct.

I hope that helps explain the special details of the story. But I realize that the miracle angle resists logical explanation.

Still, I think by now it should be obvious that Someone up there really did take a special interest in the lives of Sara and Baraq.

I have always found it odd that so many humans think of God in negative terms. And one of the most negative to me is their fondness for talking about how God tests folks by making them ill, or poor, or miserable, all in an effort to see if they really love him. God doesn't do that, of course, but humans like to think everything bad in their lives is the fault of someone else, while the good things happen because they are deserved or earned. Well, as this story shows, sometimes people need outside help— from their families (like Sara's dad or Baraq's grandfather), their teachers (like Dr. Gordon), their rabbis (like the one who taught Sara about *Shalom*), their students (like Derek and Jeff), their maids (like Carlita), animals that love and understand them—or from many other "people" who come into their lives and care about them.

I guess the most unusual part of this story is that two really smart people actually thought they were alone, when lots of folks who loved them were close at hand all along. I know if he would just think about it, Dr. Broulliette would understand that this kind of help is exactly what he means when he talks about the "godness" in the universe. Who but "God" would have sent all those caring people (plus a really smart cat and even an angel tucked away in the body of a Bullmastiff) in the first place!

At any rate, I'm especially happy to report that divine involvement in human life is a reality even when humans don't recognize it. And sometimes, good things do happen to good people. Ivory and I knew it all along, and I think Sara and Dr. Broulliette have finally been convinced.

I hope you are too.

Final Notes

This is a work of fiction. I am a Professor of Jewish Studies, and some reviewers have assumed that I am writing an autobiography. In a word, Dr. Broulliette is much smarter, more successful, brave, kind, funny, and handsome than am I. You might say that he is the Jewish Studies professor I wish I could have become somewhere other than in my dreams. I did not serve in the IDF, never was saved from death by an army canine, and am not fluent in as many languages as Dr. Broulliette.

And Sara is not a real person either. After years of single life, I tried to enter the world of internet dating sites. I met several interesting and fun ladies. But in each case, my hopes of finding the girl of my dreams fell short. None of my dating partners found me alluring, and no lasting relationship developed. I did not cease to dream, however, and when one particular dating hopeful was obviously not going to pan out, I sat down to write about what I wished could happen. I concluded that my dream was unrealistic. After all, since I was clearly far less a "catch" than Dr. Broulliette, I could hardly expect to land a real person as beautiful and charming as a real-life Sara.

My creative talent for names lags far behind most other writers. And most of the characters in the book are fictional. But I have appropriated names of some real people in my life, even though the roles they play in *The Rabbi and the Widow* are quite different from their roles in my real life. My son's name is Baraq, the first name of the hero. His middle name is David, the only son of Dr. Broulliette in the story. Nicole is my older daughter's middle name, and my younger daughter's name is Abigail. Using their real names is my way of acknowledging that they have been important in my life.

Broulliette was the maiden name of my maternal grandmother, Cyrus Gordon was my major professor in graduate studies at Brandeis University. A wonderful canine named Lilit was my first service dog, she did alert me in advance of a heart attack, and I still think of her daily ten years after her death. And I am very happily married with a beautiful widow. Shortly after we met, she found the rough draft of my manuscript on a desk in my home office and read it without my knowledge. Much to my surprise, she then announced to me that she was Sara. It was the opening gambit in a whirlwind romance that resulted in our marriage. Please do not tell her, but as far short of Dr. Broulliette as I am, that is how far beyond my fondest dream the real Sara, my wife Leslie, is. But since it is a Jewish goal to marry "up," I am not allowing her a do-over.

CPSIA information can be obtained
at www.ICGtesting.com
Printed in the USA
BVHW031410290621
610722BV00005B/578

9 781736 273968